WALLS OF INDIFFERENCE

WALLS OF INDIFFERENCE

IMMIGRATION AND THE MILITARIZATION OF THE US-MEXICO BORDER

NICOLE I. TORRES

Routledge
Taylor & Francis Group

LONDON AND NEW YORK

First published 2015 by Paradigm Publishers

Published 2016 by Routledge
2 Park Square, Milton Park, Abingdon, Oxfordshire OX14 4RN
711 Third Avenue, New York, NY 10017, USA

First issued in paperback 2016

Routledge is an imprint of the Taylor & Francis Group, an informa business

Library of Congress Cataloging-in-Publication Data

Torres, Nicole I., author.
   Walls of indifference : immigration and the militarization of the US-Mexico
border / Nicole I. Torres.
      pages cm
   Includes bibliographical references and index.
   ISBN 978-1-61205-748-4 (hardcover : alk. paper)—
   ISBN 978-1-61205-710-1 (library ebook)
   1. Arizona—Emigration and immigration.   2. Borderlands—Arizona.
3. Border security—Social aspects—Arizona.   4. Illegal aliens—Arizona—
Social conditions.   5. Social conflict—Arizona.   I. Title.
   JV6912.T67 2014
   325.73—dc23
                                                          2014019482

ISBN 13: 978-1-6120-5749-1 (pbk)
ISBN 13: 978-1-61205-748-4 (hbk)

To Mom, Randy, Nana, and the Romeros.

The Arch of Heaven

In the Name of the Son of Light,
The Son of Maria,
Foster Son of Brighd in Avalon,
Keystone of the Arch of Heaven,
He Who Joins as One,
The Forks Upholding the Sky.

His the Right Hand,
His the Left Hand,
His the Rainbow Letters,
All in Rich Fermented Milk.

We Will Go in His Name,
In All Shapes of Shapes,
In All Colors of Colors,
Upon the Path to Peace.

It is the Son of Light,
The Son of Maria, Saying
"Ask in My Name and Peace Shall be Given Unto You,"
"Enter in My Name and Ye Shall in No Wise be Cast Out."

Do You See Us Here,
Oh, Son of Light?

Says the Son of Light,
"I See!"

CONTENTS

✳

AUTHOR'S NOTE

This book is based on participation in numerous situations and conversations. It is also based on more than one hundred interviews that I conducted over the course of two and a half years. I have changed names and identifying features. In order to preserve confidentiality, some of the descriptions of individuals contain elements taken from more than one person or situation. I use generic terms such as *social worker* and *officer* in a further effort to preserve anonymity.

✳

ACKNOWLEDGMENTS

I would like to thank the following people and organizations for their support and assistance in preparing this book. I extend a very special thanks to my doctoral committee. My chair, Lorna Rhodes, supported my commitment to this project from beginning to end and gave me much needed mentoring and coaching. Daniel Hoffman and Miriam Kahn provided encouragement and exceptional feedback during my entire doctoral program, for which I am grateful. I owe a special thanks to Jason De León who introduced me to his Migrant Material Culture Project. His project illuminated my own fieldwork and strengthened my ethnographic analysis. I extend a hearty thanks to Devon Peña, Maria Elena Garcia, Eugene Aisenburg, and Juan Guerra. I am ever grateful for their support and guidance at various points in my doctoral research. I also thank the many others who have supported me, challenged me, and encouraged me during my doctoral program.

To the residents of Phoenix and Tucson who were gracious enough to tell me your stories, I express my deep gratitude. Thank you for your patience and for your willingness to share experiences that were undoubtedly painful. Although I cannot name you here, please know that I am deeply indebted to you and admire your dedication.

I would have not been able to complete this research without the financial support of the Graduate Office of Minority Affairs Program, the Stroum/Bank of America Dissertation Writing Fellowship, and the University of Washington's Anthropology Department.

Thanks to Cade, Andy, Sam, and Moss for your feedback and willingness to listen to my stories about fieldwork. I extend a special thanks to the Pick and family. Mom, Randy, Grandma, Nana, and Dad, this book is the product of your unwavering support from *el barrio*—the 'hood. My last and best thanks are to my partner, Gary Moore, who has untiringly supported me in this research during the past four years through all the editing, sleepless nights, and countless cups of coffee.

Introduction

Arizona and the Ecology of Militarization

On January 8, 2011, at approximately 10:00 a.m., Arizona congresswoman Gabrielle Giffords was shot during one of her local "Meet and Greet" events. This occurred in the parking lot of a Safeway supermarket in the Tucson metropolitan area. The shooter, Jared Lee Loughner, injured fourteen bystanders and killed six people—including a local district court judge.

The Tucson shooting, as it is now called, took place during the final days of my dissertation fieldwork in Arizona. At the time it occurred, I was talking with Dan, a friend of mine who ran a local bed and breakfast (B&B). As I stood in his kitchen, I listened to him reflect on the social climate of Arizona, the politics surrounding the US-Mexico border, and immigration. Dan complained that the current political climate around the border and immigration policy did not encourage "holistic thinking," something he considered to be vital. According to Dan, the construction of the US-Mexico border "creates war" and "makes it hard to solve problems," to the point where "no one is safe."

The dovetailing of Dan's comments and the Tucson shooting goes to the very heart of my project: What kinds of environments assemble the conditions that make violence possible? This question emerged from my interest in prison populations; I was curious as to what variables, besides race and class, led to incarceration. Ultimately, this question led me to Arizona. I learned that border politics, public conversations regarding immigration, detention centers, gated communities, and the people themselves encompass multiple topographies. These topographies, as I explain, compose what I call the ecology of militarization.

This ethnography documents and explores the social, political, and material consequences of militarization in the borderlands of Arizona. Based on two years of fieldwork in Phoenix, Tucson, and along the US-Mexico border, I identify militarization as a social and political phenomenon that gradually reconfigures both individuals and communities. What is most striking about the process of militarization is its instrumentalization. Although fieldwork participants use the tropes of immigration and race as central points for discussion, I observed that these discourses point to a much broader trend of social, psychological, and political transformation connected to the proliferation of vigilantism, gated communities, and detention centers. Most recently, this transformation is embodied and articulated through the experiences of *border crossers*—men, women, and children who enter the United States without authorization due to multiple factors, including socioeconomic constraints.[1] Most crossers enter the United States looking specifically for work. However, many also cross the border hoping to reunite with family members who work in the United States and who can no longer risk returning to Mexico or other parts of Latin America.

Over the course of the last two decades, and especially since September 11, 2001, federal border enforcement has become far more rigorous and oppressive. Border enforcement in urbanized areas has higher levels of surveillance, whereas desert areas lack rigorous security. Consequently, these desert areas attract more unauthorized travelers desiring to enter the United States, despite being more hazardous to cross. Federal government officials rationalized that the desert itself would naturally restrict the flow of crossers, a strategy known as "Prevention Through Deterrence (PTD)."[2] However, this strategy has not succeeded, and despite the fifty-mile trek, people continue to cross the border through the harsh terrain of the Sonoran Desert. Thus Arizona holds a unique position as a border state, acting as a funnel for migrants crossing the border surreptitiously.

Migrants who decide to cross the border by foot through the vast Sonoran Desert unwittingly place themselves at multiple levels of risk. Those who hire the "assistance" of a coyote (paid human smuggler) risk being exploited through financial extortion, threats to family in their country of origin, and, especially for women, sexual coercion. Because of the difficult terrain and extreme temperatures characteristic of the desert, individuals who choose to cross risk their lives. Although some migrants pay a significant amount for human smuggling, others who are unable to afford the services of a coyote resort to crossing the desert without an escort, thus putting themselves at even greater danger. They are often unaware of the exceptional hazards involved and are unprepared for the length and severity of the journey. Travelers run out of food and water, suffer from debilitating blisters, and endure venomous bites. No longer able to walk, some crossers become stranded and die. Depending on the time of year, migrants may experience hypothermia, hyperthermia, dehydration, heat exhaustion, or heatstroke. Since 1999, thousands of people have died miserably while attempting to cross the desert.[3]

In Arizona, the gruesome deaths of border crossers have emerged as a humanitarian and environmental quandary. For the spectrum of local

Figure I   Posters and T-shirts on sale at a local rally in Phoenix.

activists who advocate for what they view as the fundamental human rights of border crossers, the deaths in the desert represent an egregious violation of human rights. When I met humanitarian activists, they frequently started conversations with the cry, "People are dying out in the desert!" Horrified by what they see as the flagrant indifference to the deaths of migrants, these activists constitute several groups of tireless individuals who are dedicated to saving the lives of border crossers. The activists I encountered worked in a range of community-based activities; many habitually collected money to purchase food, socks, water, blankets, communication equipment, and first aid supplies for migrants in need. Tucson-based members regularly patrolled the desert looking for any crossers who were lost, injured, or stranded. Activists in the large urban areas of Phoenix and Tucson focused on policy change and implementation, racial profiling, and faith-based activities, and some emphasized indigenous rights and self-determination. All of these individuals were extremely dedicated to their cause. Despite the

**Figure 2   Border enforcement supporters
at a public protest in Phoenix.**

fact that many activists were not financially well off, they frequently spent what little money they had to purchase goods and services that supported their humanitarian activities. Their level of dedication and ongoing struggle have justifiably gained them international attention and admiration.

Yet many residents of Phoenix and Tucson respond to the migrants' tales of hardship and death with indifference. They complain that Arizona is now a "funnel" for migrants, which protects other states from the influx of border crossers. Phoenix and Tucson now serve as way stations for migrants who are traveling to their final destinations, and many residents in these cities are increasingly troubled by the growth of migrant populations in their communities. Although unauthorized migration is merely a civil offense, individuals who support border enforcement see migrants as *criminals* and as *illegal aliens* who deserve the harsh consequences of crossing the desert's hostile landscape, being caught and imprisoned, or dying of exposure. They view border crossers as trespassers who brazenly violate international laws and as dirty people who *trash* the United States with impunity. These residents are critical of the PTD strategy and interpret the federal government's policy as a form of malign neglect, insisting that the government has abandoned them. Angered by the audacity of border crossers and their willingness to *break into* the United States and violate its laws, these citizens have chosen to take matters into their own hands. A number of vigilante and citizen-action groups have emerged that focus on migrant deterrence, border wall fortification, and citizen policing. With their formation, the social and political landscape of Arizona now mirrors the extremities found in the physical climate and geographic terrain, and their activities have gained international notoriety.

Arizona is a landlocked state and shares its 389-mile southern border[4] with the Mexican states of Sonora and Baja California. It has a rugged terrain and an extremely dry climate that is usually classified as arid or semi-arid. The Sonoran Desert embraces both Tucson and Phoenix, the state's capital. However, the desert itself crosses the border, reaching into the Mexican states of Sonora, Sinaloa, and Baja California. The rough geography and dry climate often serve as metaphors for the larger political debates that take place in the state. Residents call the summer heat of Arizona *oppressive* and human rights activists see parallels between this and the sentiments of those who support border enforcement. My

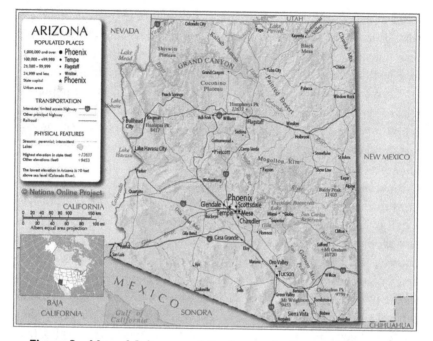

Figure 3   Map of Arizona and the border it shares with Mexico.

research participants, especially those in Phoenix with its record-breaking summer temperatures, described Arizona in biblical terms, calling it *Hell, desolate, Dante's Inferno,* and *the lake of fire.* During my visits, I frequently saw a bumper sticker that read, "Arizona: It's a dry hate." The more time I spent in Arizona, the more I understood why people paired the heat and dryness of the landscape with the harsh and inflammatory politics of immigration. I realized that the militarization of the US-Mexico border was not something that was simply happening "out there"; rather, I began to see that it had deep social, physical, and psychological effects on the individuals I met.

Theorizing the Border as "Statecraft"

Many discussions of militarization in the United States center on the US-Mexico border. The border wall—a sprawling 1,969 miles long that

Figure 4   Sign in the window of a local bookstore in Tucson.

stretches from California to Texas—is an especially contested topic. In Arizona, there are avid supporters of the wall, intense detractors, vigilante groups, self-proclaimed humanitarian groups, and those who remain ambivalent. Although many individuals in the United States have an opinion about the border wall and assume they know what takes place there, few have any reason to visit the borderlands and know little other than what they see and hear via television, the Internet, and other media.

Although the United States shares a border with Canada, the strategies for enforcing that border are less baroque and emphasize technological solutions. This results, as one Border Patrol officer explained, from "all the manpower being dedicated to securing the US-Mexico border." Yet as many government officials have noted, the border wall is ineffective. As Janet Napolitano, the former governor of Arizona and current secretary of Homeland Security, said, "You show me a 50-foot wall and I'll show you a 51-foot ladder at the border. That's the way the border works."[5] If that's true, then why are individuals enchanted by the notion of a fortified border wall? Perhaps a public display of defense and surveillance along the US-Mexico border offers citizens an idealized view of the United States as a sovereign, cohesive country. It might suggest that government has full control over its border and is able to protect its citizens from unwanted others, especially those to the south. For example, since the attack on the World Trade Center on September 11, 2001, a crucial part of strengthening the image of the nation has been the deployment of media strategies and imagery to encourage a perception of victory, such as George W. Bush's "Mission Accomplished" speech, which implied that the United States was winning the war in Iraq and that the war was coming to an end.

Such public displays of power are one aspect of a political practice called *statecraft*. The political scientist Peter Andreas defines the art of statecraft as the art of attaining political power through the social management of citizens. It relies on a continuous process of nation-building by which "the state must constantly reproduce boundaries (spatial, social, cultural, economic, and political) between 'us' and 'them.'"[6] Andreas argues that US-Mexico border policies are similar to Erving Goffman's theory of impression management; border policy must embody a dual performance, "assuring the border be opened to legal flows," yet simultaneously "sufficiently closed to illegal flows."[7] Thus the border becomes an elaborate ceremonial practice of social distinction focused on citizenship and belonging. This ritual practice has resulted in baroque policing and paramilitary tactics that

Figure 5   US-Mexico border, Nogales, Arizona.

Andreas identifies as *feedback effects*. These consist of an increase in the militarization of the border, the social construction of a category of illegal immigrants, and increasing rates of incarceration among undocumented individuals.[8] Although militarization and border surveillance deter some individuals from entering the country, temporary deterrence does not necessarily prevent them from attempting to return at a future date. Because border regulation occurs "largely on the basis of symbolic merits, border interdiction has become not simply a means to an end (in reducing the drug supply) but also an end in itself."[9] Andreas further observes that the

> unprecedented expansion about border policing has ultimately been less about achieving the stated instrumental goal of deterring illegal border crossers and more about politically recrafting the image of the border and symbolically reaffirming the state's territorial authority.[10]

This points to the paradoxical nature of border realities and statecraft: the state must continually inscribe and redefine its territorial authority, yet the US-Mexico border continues to be socially and spatially permeable. This continual intensification of reinscription has resulted in an increase in surveillance on both city and state levels. I contend, for example, that the *war zone* my research participants describe is the result of statecraft. Departing slightly from Andreas's conceptualization of *statecraft*, I define the term to also include the *psychological management* of members of the state. Historian Ioan Couliano described contemporary Western states as "magician" states that require the psychic reconfiguration of an individual's identity, one that is largely dependent on the deployment of symbolic and material instruments that shape membership, affinities, and senses of belonging within the nation-state.[11] Although individuals are shaped by national solidarity, they also share what one research participant described as an "indifference" to the social, psychological, and physical distress of others. In other words, statecraft requires that individuals become accustomed to, or actively participate in, the social and physical distress of others. My approach to statecraft is thus in accordance with what the political scientist Achille Mbembe observes: the central project of the state is "the generalized instrumentalization of human existence and the material destruction of human bodies and populations."[12] Based on my fieldwork, I suggest that militarization is an essential component of this process and indeed is how violence is organized at the level of the state.

The Ecology of Militarization and the Institutionalization of Violence

In this book I examine the discourses of illegal immigration, race, border fortification, and crime as specific components of a larger ecology of militarization. The framework of my analysis loosely draws upon anthropologist Gregory Bateson's discussion of an *ecology of mind*. Bateson was a founder of systems theory and was arguably the most influential anthropologist within this theoretical framework. His discussion of an ecology of mind, or as he later states, an "ecology of ideas" engages with a basic question: *How do ideas interact?* This argument that there is indeed an ecology of ideas, which mutually inform and shape one another, points to a fundamental anthropological tenet in my project: within any social system there is an internal cultural logic at work. Bateson looks at the interaction of ideas holistically; for any given situation, the way ideas are exchanged and circulated results in tangible social and material consequences. Accordingly, the repeated exchange and articulation of certain ideas produces a kind of *metabolism* in the environment. The ecology of militarization centers on how ideas interact and ultimately shape the behavior of human beings, their environment, and their collective sense of self—thus, how individuals perceive what they consider to be reality. In other words, militarization is not simply something that happens along the border; instead, in places like Phoenix and Tucson, militarization is woven to varying degrees into every detail of daily life. Individuals like Dan, quoted at the beginning of this chapter, acknowledge that there is an ecological component to the process of militarization. For Dan and other participants, militarization is a process that is socially shaped and *socially shaping*. In the case of Arizona, militarization is a part of the political geography of the borderlands; it directly influences the phenomenon of migration and strongly contributes to the thousands of deaths that have occurred in the borderlands over the past two decades. Consequently, I am concerned with how practices of militarization relate to two interrelated phenomena: (1) how militarization operates as a system and a process, and (2) what technologies enable individuals to adapt to violence and become indifferent to the social and physical death of others.

The anthropologist Catherine Lutz describes militarization as the activities and rhetoric produced by "war preparation" that is "the legacy and rhetoric of national security."[13] Although this description is useful, I contend that processes of militarization go beyond preparing for war and conceptualizations of national security. Although those things are indeed part of the ecology of militarization, the entire constellation of militarization is fundamentally ecological: it depends on an assemblage of social and cultural practices, such as language, socialization, and the creation and manipulation of material objects. Thus, I argue that what people in Phoenix and Tucson have begun to describe as the process of militarization is actually part of a larger social process through which violence is institutionalized. My approach supports ethnoecologist Devon Peña's assertion regarding contemporary political demarcations. He states, "we have drawn too hard a line between people and the environment," whereby social, cultural, and centuries-old interactions of people and place are disregarded by modern nation-states that result in the displacement and disenfranchisement of entire populations.[14] One effect of this hard line is the institutionalization of violence.

Institutionalized violence in Arizona has a long history that precedes the creation of the state itself. Arizona has always had a place in the US collective imagination as a borderline state, both literally and metaphorically. It is located on the edges of a national geography where nation-making, war-making, rigidity, and lawlessness converge and create the conditions of possibility for violence to erupt. Like its neighboring states, Arizona is a direct descendant of colonialism. Even prior to the US-Mexico War in 1846, these border states were what Ann Stoler describes as landscapes of "ruin and ruination," geographic zones configured in ways that exacerbate individual and collective suffering.[15] Long-term practices of statecraft are rooted in self-conscious national myth-making narratives, such as frontier individualism and freedom, the *land of opportunity,* Manifest Destiny, the destruction of indigenous populations, and strategically deployed notions of class and race. Therefore, I examine how the contemporary immigration debate relies on a specific interaction of ideas: the rhetoric of nationalism, class differences, and the language of war. These discursive techniques are conflated in a way that suppresses the opportunity for any alternative positions to emerge. Thus, the *immigration debate* is a superficial performance of a predicament that has deep roots; it is an example of how public debates both conceal and reveal long-standing systemic problems.

Although I investigate processes of militarization, I simultaneously explore (1) the deleterious effects of the language of the war on immigration and (2) contemporary conceptions of race and racism; these themes permeated the linguistic terrain of Arizona, and especially that of Phoenix residents. Predominately academic conceptualizations of race and related discourses, such as *whiteness,* are now popularized and have become useful in some contexts. However, these discussions are now hegemonic and reinscribe the social categories inherent in racialized discussions and suppress alternative analyses and strategies. Through this process, individuals participate in fixing racial categories, thus making ethnoracial categorizations static. When individuals attach themselves to these static categories, this enlists them to do what I describe as the *work of the state.* This work, appearing as militarization, results in a social and environmental situation that residents speak of as *war.* In the state capital of Phoenix, which is nearly 300 miles away from the US-Mexico border, militarization is not an occurrence *on the border;* instead, it is a specific state of mind through which people have socially and psychologically adapted to varying levels of structural and interpersonal violence.

To understand how individuals adapt to varying degrees of violence, I employ Slavoj Žižek's analysis. Žižek untangles the ways in which violence, the direct or indirect phenomenon of injury, operates on three intertwined levels: subjective, objective, and systemic. Žižek argues that subjective violence, or "violence performed by a clearly identifiable agent," is the most obvious and the kind that draws the most attention. But as he explains,

> subjective violence is just the most visible portion of a triumvirate that includes two objective kinds of violence. First, there is a "symbolic" violence embodied in language and its forms, what Heidegger would call "our house of being." ... Second, there is what I call "systemic" violence, or the often catastrophic consequences of the smooth functioning of our economic and political systems.[16]

In other words, subjective violence stands in contrast to the "'normal,' peaceful state of things," the social and systemic space where other forms of violence are routinized and invisible. To varying degrees, these three forms of violence are accepted in daily life: *subjective* (direct); *symbolic,* such as discrimination; and *systemic,* such as political and economic patterns of destruction. Žižek argues that this triumvirate of violence is so tightly interwoven that it "blunts our ability to see"[17] the less visible forms of violence—specifically the symbolic and systemic forms that are part of our daily lives.

The normalization and institutionalization of violence are what Žižek describes as the "fascination of subjective violence."[18] He sees this fascination as a social tendency that individuals should resist. This is an enchantment that distracts us from understanding how subjective violence is connected to the other two forms of violence. When individuals fixate on subjective violence, it occludes the other forms of violence and results in the overall production of violence, a phenomenon that cuts across any perceived racial or ethnic boundaries. There is no *winner* in this social configuration. Rather, what profits most from this occlusion of violence are capitalism and the nation-state. The research participants with whom I spoke in Arizona were all casualties of a war, albeit not the war on immigration. Instead they are the recent casualties of globalized capitalism, living in a state that grew exponentially during the housing boom of the mid-1990s and suffered drastically during the turn of the twenty-first century housing bust. Arizona, a state where the government's administration had to sell off state buildings to resolve its fiscal woes, tends to be socially, historically, and financially stigmatized.[19] Bankruptcy and foreclosure billboards litter the landscape with such a frequency that a friend of mine visiting Arizona remarked, "This just goes to show the absurdity of modern life." Symptoms of the state's ongoing distress, the signs are visual records of a pervasive misery that psychically affects all individuals, albeit in different ways.

The consequences of this distress manifested themselves most recently on April 23, 2010, when Governor Jan Brewer signed the Support Our Law Enforcement and Safe Neighborhoods Act (SB 1070).[20] Critics argue that this bill encourages racial profiling by the police and targets anyone perceived to be of Latino descent. Activists who support migrants consider the bill to be another attack on the dignity of an already vulnerable population. Media pundits, activists, and academics generally point to events like these as proof of what they consider to be anti-immigration

Figure 6   Sign in local bar, downtown Tucson.

sentiment. However, the social and economic distress, deterioration, and dysfunctional relationships reveal something other than the immigration debate. Borrowing from Žižek's analysis, I have observed that a particular *house of being*—namely, militarization—emerges from the social world of

Arizona. Militarization includes an ever-expanding list of concerns and grievances that include racism, war, downward mobility, crime, drugs, illegality, citizenship and belonging, arguments of indigeneity, class divisions, ethnoracial categories, and political affiliations.

Thus, I investigate how individuals become both subjects and agents in these processes of militarization. I depart from Cynthia Enloe's original definition to understand militarization as a "step-by-step process by which a person or thing gradually comes to be controlled by the military,"[21] recognizing that militarization shapes an individual's "inner space," where it functions as a "strategic set of psychological border operations"[22] aimed at the internalization and production of violence. Based on this understanding, the chapters of this book address how, through five specific technologies of governance, individuals adapt to the discourse of war and the militarization of their communities as subjects of, and participants in, what legal scholar Jonathan Simon describes as *governing through crime*. These practices, which are necessary for governing through crime, are fundamental to the social and psychological conditions necessary for militarization to develop. With this foundational understanding of militarization, I investigate how the accompanying processes become practiced and embodied. The phenomenon of militarization is difficult to identify precisely because its practices are so deeply embedded in our everyday lives. We suffer from what Louis Althusser describes as "interpellation." According to Althusser, because ideology is "everywhere" and "eternal," even the pre-ideological individual is instantly transformed into a subject proper. Therefore, "individuals are always-already subjects."[23] They are socialized around the ideas and practices essential to militarization and thus are unable to identify them as ideological. Through these processes militarization becomes systematized and nearly invisible.

Fieldwork, Methods, and Definitions

From December 2008 to January 2011, I traveled between Arizona and Seattle, Washington (where I currently live), to conduct my research. My work initially began in Phoenix where I explored the ongoing effects of what I initially understood as the *war on immigration*. Eventually, my interviewees pointed me to Tucson where I spent considerable time with activists, accompanying them on their patrols in the Sonoran Desert while they looked for border crossers in need of aid. My methodology involved sixty-eight structured interviews with residents in the Phoenix and Tucson metropolitan areas. The interviewees included a range of people: those who were born and raised in Arizona, residents who considered themselves *transplants* from other states, local politicians, undocumented migrants,[24] government employees, and people who self-identified as *activists*. I followed up on the structured interviews with about forty semi-structured interviews with key participants who represented the range of social, political, and economic variance among my fieldwork population. Nearly all of my initial interviews were gained through snowball sampling: I cultivated relationships with a variety of individuals who then referred me to others they thought would be willing to speak with me.

The majority of my interviews were conducted in English (most participants, regardless of ethnicity, were fluent or proficient in English), a few in both English and Spanish, and one exclusively in Spanish. All names presented here are pseudonyms.[25] During each interview, I took handwritten notes that I recorded by number; I did not link identifiers with the data. I also conducted participant observation in a wide variety of settings: functions and events at civic institutions, political protests and rallies, local events focused on hate speech and immigration policy, fund-raising events, arts events, trips with humanitarian aid volunteers to the Sonoran Desert, attendance at immigration court, tours of detention centers, and attendance at town hall meetings in the Phoenix metropolitan area.

One of the challenges I experienced during my research was the use of categories. Although categories help us explain and organize the world in which we live, these categories have the potential to become identities— ways in which individuals make and unmake the world, assign attributes, and allow for militarization to emerge. During fieldwork, I noticed that dependency among participants on categories of affiliation and affinity often resulted in contradictory subjective understandings. For example, a person connected to a specific event may be classified in a multiplicity of ways, depending on who is narrating the story or attempting to *make* the world at that moment. This was most evident with the two categories of *illegal immigrant* and *undocumented migrant*. Individuals who self-identified as *patriots and citizens* who are *concerned with the rule of law,* used the phrase *illegal immigrant* to describe individuals who crossed the US-Mexico border and lacked formal documentation. People who used this phrase were in support of border enforcement and stressed the need for formal membership in the nation-state. This category focused on the notions of *citizenship and belonging.* Meanwhile, individuals who desired comprehensive immigration policy reform that emphasized amnesty and a more open border policy used the phrases *undocumented migrant, undocumented worker,* or *unauthorized migrant.* They emphasized the ordinariness of migration between geographically contiguous political entities and stressed the need for a focus on *human welfare* and a *humanitarian approach* in reforms and policy making for the US-Mexico border. The individuals who subscribed to this perspective identified themselves as *progressives* and *humanitarians.* In addition to the progressives and humanitarians, other groups that rejected categorizations based on the nation-state were activists who challenged the narrative of the nation-state and did not subscribe to the construction or legitimacy of geopolitical borders. These individuals usually self-identified as *Chicano* and/or *indigenous.* They were concerned with human welfare, autonomy, restoration of homelands, and liberation from imperial forces.

As the ethnographic narrator of this particular story, I recognize that the terms *illegal immigrant, undocumented worker,* and *indigenous* stem from particular positions within historiography, and they necessarily produce certain kinds of history. I subscribe to Michel-Rolph Trouillot's understanding of history in which "the boundary between what has happened and that which is said to have happened is necessary," but also "ambiguous and contingent."[26] Thus I have consciously chosen to use the term *border crosser* to represent individuals who recognize that they are traveling from one political jurisdiction to another and through this process experience a sense of liminality. They are on the threshold of life and death, neither here nor there, in the no-man's land of the harsh Sonoran Desert. Border crossers are perceived as criminals and lack the legal protection that rests on citizenship. Moreover, the individuals with whom I spoke who had migrated across the boundary between the United States and Mexico described themselves as "crossing the border." Although the term *border crosser* is also a contested term, in my experience it is the least problematic of the four. The greatest resistance toward this phrase comes from Chicano and indigenous activists. They are usually American citizens of mixed ancestry who argue, "We didn't cross the border—the border crossed us!" This argument is unquestionably valid. Nevertheless, I deliberately choose to use the term *border crosser*. I use it to denote the social and political transformation that occurs when an individual decides to move from one political jurisdiction to another, a process I describe in Chapter 5. I use *border crosser* to convey the radical nature of the act itself. By risking their lives, individuals also provide a commentary on the oppressive conditions under which they have been living. People who resort to crossing the border do so under the most extreme of circumstances. They participate in an embodied performance that expresses the dysfunction of the current geopolitical conditions. This performance reveals that current configurations of nation-states in North America are *states of injury*, regimes that harm and debilitate their citizen-subjects. When border crossers, under extreme distress, leave objects behind or eventually die in the desert, they become a public record and a testament to the apathy of local and national governments.

While in the field, I, too, became the subject of social and political stereotyping and scrutiny. This inspection stemmed from my position as a Puerto Rican and as an academic. I received the most social acceptance from individuals who considered themselves progressives. In each encounter I experienced among progressives, humanitarians, and Chicano/indigenous activists, they automatically considered me one of their own in defense of liberal, or what they considered to be morally just, causes. My last name, Torres, gave me an automatic pass into the realm of progressive and humanitarian causes. Most people I encountered assumed I was either Mexican or from a Latin American country south of the border. In contrast, I found it extremely challenging to obtain interviews with individuals who were in support of border enforcement. I was immediately incorporated into local ecologies: my identity as a researcher and an academic seemed to be code for *biased liberal*. Regardless of their ethnicity, activists and other individuals who were in support of border enforcement and deportation were the least likely to speak with me, although some of them did.

A Caveat on Categories, Especially Racial Ones

Although I question the usefulness of racial categories and alliances, I do not dismiss experiences of discrimination based on racialization. I am fully aware of the profound effects of interpersonal discrimination; it is through everyday encounters of discrimination that institutional racism becomes a powerful *force*.[27] However, I am skeptical of the ways in which discussions that are centered on race have become totalizing explanations that silence other modes of analysis. Here, I distance myself from mainstream understandings of race and instead consider it part of an unquestioned "distinctive ecology of belonging."[28] As I demonstrate, race as an analytic category and an explanatory instrument (and its auxiliary discourses, such as whiteness) has become *the* master narrative among my fieldwork participants in Arizona. This discourse is so entrenched and unyielding that it results in a truly ironic predicament. In their attempts to eradicate racism, activists and policymakers use the discourse of race as an explanatory model for the immigration debate. However, the discourse of race totalizes and polarizes to such an extent that it actually thwarts attempts to eradicate racism. This dynamic is especially evident among political progressives and humanitarian activists. I argue that this discourse is a technology of governance. It provides the conditions of possibility necessary for the process of militarization to take place and further enables statecraft.

Chapter Overviews—Contraptions of Statecraft

Each chapter is an examination of *contraptions*,[29] or the extravagant devices that are essential to statecraft. These devices assist in the reconfiguration of the social, political, and psychological landscape and allow for the emergence of militarization. In Chapter 1, I provide a basic overview of three main threads of Arizona history from which the current social and political climate of Arizona emerged. They include (1) Arizona as a central figure in the narratives of crime and punishment that have proliferated in the United States; (2) the mythology of the Wild West as a defining component in the shaping of Arizona's place in US history; and

(3) antiunion activism at the turn of the twentieth century and the definition of what it means to be *American*. I tie these threads together to help the reader understand how these historical conditions have helped to cultivate contemporary discussions of illegality, criminality, and war around the US-Mexico border.

Chapter 2 charts out how the language of war functions as a technology of governance. Through ethnographic examples, I explore how the vocabularies of race, nationalism, and patriotism are devices of depoliticization. I argue that these vocabularies repress class awareness and examine how racialized discourses actually reveal anxieties related to social and economic marginalization. I argue that the language of nationalism and patriotism offers a sense of belonging, affinity, and protection to stigmatized, downwardly mobile individuals who feel, as one woman described, as if "they have nowhere else to go." By using the language of patriotism and fixating on immigration as a problem, downwardly mobile citizens recruit themselves into the project of statecraft.

In Chapter 3, I demonstrate how *governing through crime* is instrumentalized within the borderlands of Arizona. I argue that governing through crime is simultaneously state-making and subject-making, as well as a process that relies on the discourse of illegal immigration to operate throughout society. Individuals are trained to identify *criminals* and ethnoracial others as unproductive subjects of the state. These constructions associated with state power depend heavily on how individuals manage and construct their own identities—a matter I further explore in Chapter 4.

Chapter 4 explores how the interior landscapes of individuals are operationalized so that they work on behalf of the state. I draw on the work of psychologist Marsha Linehan to describe the social and political impasse that permeates the terrain of both Phoenix and Tucson. By applying Linehan's understanding of dialectical failure, I analyze how the borderland areas of Arizona are contested terrains and geographies of anguish. I examine the experiences of the now infamous Arizona residents Jared Lee Loughner and Shawna Forde to demonstrate that these geographies of anguish are testaments to what Ann Stoler identifies as the process of *ruination*—that is, the continuing deleterious effects of imperialism on both persons and places. Ruination results in the incoherence and eventual breakdown of both local and national governance, which my participants identify as *war*.

Consequently, the potential emerges for citizen-subjects to increase their participation in statecraft by functioning as soldiers of war.

In Chapter 5, I explore the effects of statecraft and examine its social, physical, and psychological consequences. I argue that physical encampments and social exclusion are the formative components of Giorgio Agamben's description of the *death camp.* The camp is preceded by what Gilroy describes as *camp thinking,* a psychic landscape where subjects assist in the social and physical death of others. I also explore how individuals create social artifacts—physical objects—and build their communities in ways that extend and reinforce statecraft. When we examine both the ideas and the objects that are mechanisms of statecraft, they reveal anxieties that many residents share about the social and economic breakdown of local communities and the nation.

Chapter 6 is a visual ethnography. I use photographs to chronicle the harsh realms that border crossers traverse, including both the hostile physical landscape and the inflammatory social and political debates. The photos are a visual journey through these multiple topographies. The photographs examine narratives of race, crime, migrancy, indigeneity, and the continuing deleterious effects of colonialism.

Finally, in the conclusion, I argue that the social suffering that my research illuminates is the social and material consequence of statecraft. Both residents and those who travel through the borderlands live along the fault lines of the nation-state and are habituated to conflict through the militarization of their communities. Left in an unceasing state of injury, many individuals who live in borderlands of Arizona suffer from a devastating condition that permeates their habitats and consumes them both physically and psychologically. I end by examining militarization as a socioecological process, arguing that by reconfiguring the sense of self, it conditions citizens to do the necessary labor of statecraft. Thus are they trained toward indifference to human suffering and destruction on the intertwined dimensions of the person, the region, and the nation.

CHAPTER 1
ARIZONA AND ITS "CONDITIONS OF POSSIBILITY"

> It's a violation of the criminal law to come across the
> border and be here. They are criminals—illegal.
> —*Sheriff Joseph Arpaio*[1]

One Sunday morning, when I was about to sit down to write a conference paper, my research on Arizona began. I planned to write a paper that addressed what factors, besides race, contributed to the "carceral dragnet." Arizona was the farthest thing from my mind; I had no interest in going there. It was too hot, too harsh, and too far south for my taste. I decided to turn on the radio; I needed some background noise to help me focus my writing. Suddenly, I heard voices shouting, "Illegals go home!" and "Criminals!" This radio show turned out to be a feature piece regarding Arizona, the epicenter of the immigration debate. This developed into a long and arduous two and a half years of dissertation research.

Joseph Arpaio, the notorious sheriff of Maricopa County, was featured on that show. Pundits and allies alike describe him as policing Maricopa County with a new twist on the "war on terror." Since September 11, 2001, Arpaio—who refers to himself as "America's Toughest Sheriff"—has adopted a stricter stance against immigration across the US-Mexico border. Maricopa County, home to the state capital of Phoenix, is *the* touchstone for the ongoing local and national debates that the 9/11 "war on terror" initiated in local political discussions. With a Latino population of approximately 30 percent and a considerable migrant population from Latin America, the county is currently known as "Ground Zero" for the immigration debate. This debate has greatly intensified over the last two decades, particularly since 9/11. Consequently, social critics, activists, and civilians eventually incorporated the conversation on the "war on terror" into the "war on immigration."[2]

Critics claim that Sheriff Arpaio does far more than target migrant populations; they say that the sheriff is racist and actively encourages racial profiling. Although Arpaio is the most recognized figure in the recent incarnation of the immigration debate, he is by no means the first to target migrant and border crosser populations in Arizona. As the most visible figure of Arizona law enforcement, Arpaio is only the most recent embodiment of the ways in which the politics of immigration intersect with class differences, histories of war between the United States and Mexico, and long-standing narratives of crime. The state of Arizona is characterized by an environment where historical and political events intersect to nurture hostility, conflict, and violence. Furthermore, it is a state that has a special place in the collective imagination of the United States. As home to the "Wild West," Arizona—with its notorious city of Tombstone, the place "too tough to die"—represents frontier individualism, stubbornness, and a sensibility that is the embodiment of the American Old West. Over the course of its history, Arizona has been a site pervaded with conflict and volatility.

My goal in this chapter is to trace what Michel Foucault calls *conditions of possibility,* the social and historical threads that have allowed current views on crime, immigration, and belonging to emerge. First, I give a brief overview of the social and political climate of Arizona. This genealogy is not exhaustive; rather, I focus briefly on three main themes of Arizona's history: punishment and incarceration, the mythological themes of the Wild West and frontier individualism, and finally, a basic outline of the Arizona labor movement at the turn of the twentieth century. I close with an overview of contemporary social movements and labor organizing that connects to these themes. This includes the legacy of Cesar Chavez, the prominent Mexican American civil rights activist who cofounded the United Farm Workers' Union. These historical threads help to generate the varying degrees of conflict that emerge in Arizona today.

"Sunbelt Justice": Detention, Incarceration, and Punishment

Arizona is a social and political landscape fraught with contradictions. The paradox I found most perplexing was the mistrust of "big government" found among some participants on both sides of the political spectrum. Despite the state's long-standing focus on states' rights and "fiscal frugality," Arizona is at the center of the "get tough" model of incarceration and punishment. In *Sunbelt Justice: Arizona and the American Transformation of Punishment,* criminologist Mona Lynch states that the rate of imprisonment in Arizona "ballooned from a low of 75 per 100,000 citizens in 1971 to 515 per 100,000 by the turn of the twenty-first century. . . . In every year since 1984 to the present, Arizona has been among the top 10 of the 50 states for their rates of incarceration."[3]

The state's orientation toward incarceration and punishment is part of a trend that critics describe as the *prison-industrial complex.* The prison-industrial complex is defined as a "set of bureaucratic, political, and economic interests that encourage increased spending on imprisonment, regardless of the actual need."[4] The term is derived from President Eisenhower's warning regarding the *military-industrial complex,* which he described as the "immense military establishment and large arms industry" whose "total influence—economic, political, even spiritual—is felt in every city, every State house, every office of the Federal government."[5] He believed that the military-industrial complex was a grave threat to the democratic process and to every citizen's civil liberties.[6]

Arizona holds a unique position in the development of the prison-industrial complex and its descendant, the *homeland-security-industrial complex.* Senator Barry Goldwater, a central figure whom historians and politicians credit with revitalizing the contemporary American conservative movement, was born in Phoenix, Arizona. What is now labeled as the *New Right* began with Goldwater's presidential campaign in 1964. In its earlier days, Goldwater's political orientation was perceived by the American majority to be "extreme and even dangerous."[7] However, in 1964, Goldwater, then a senator from Arizona, became famous for running a presidential campaign that used the fear of crime to attract mainstream voters, predominately white—and it worked. Although Goldwater lost the presidential election, in subsequent decades, the theme of being *tough on crime* became a central focus in political campaigns. Politicians from across the political spectrum adopted the rhetoric of being tough on crime and the public's desire for safety as touchstones in their campaigns to garner votes.[8] Over the course of fifty years, Goldwater's political sentiments and the politics of the New Right were incorporated into mainstream thinking, and they are now part of the national discourse.[9]

Goldwater's political legacy and Arizona's current penal practices are part of a local ethos of strict punishment described as *Sunbelt Justice*. According to Mona Lynch, Sunbelt Justice is based on a "distinct set of cultural norms and practices that is associated with the Sunbelt states during the second half of the twentieth century. . . . Their development is closely tied to the emergence of new post–World War II economies, such as military bases and weapons industries, air transportation, electronics and computer technology, and expanded service industries."[10] Sunbelt cities like Phoenix are characterized by suburban sprawl and low-density single-family homes (such as in the suburbs of Mesa, Chandler, Gilbert, and Scottsdale). These areas are fairly homogenous, populated by individuals who share similar social and political values.

The groundwork for the emergence of Sunbelt Justice and the New Right was laid even prior to Goldwater's arrival as a politician. Arizona, the last of the contiguous states to enter the union, is historically marked as in opposition to governmental oversight. In fact, the current emphasis on limited taxes, small government, and an ongoing suspicion of "outsiders," originates from the time when Arizona was a territory. The Arizona ethos emerges from a political environment that has its roots in "southern traditionalistic values . . . individualism, self-reliance, and self-governance."[11] This ethos is based on mythological narratives of origin and Wild West stories that many participants casually refer to in everyday conversation. "America's Toughest Sheriff," Joseph Arpaio, routinely uses these narratives.

Arizona, Arpaio, and the "Wild West"

During my first visit to Arizona, one participant exclaimed in frustration, "Nicole, it's the Wild West out here. People wear their guns in coffee shops. Coffee shops! The sheriff [Joseph Arpaio] has tanks and takes them out for the parades. I mean fucking tanks!" Participants used the phrase *Wild West* so regularly that I began to understand it as shorthand for the state's affinity for individualism, guns, and the harsh landscape. Eventually, I stopped counting how many times it was used to describe the social climate of Phoenix. Once, in a faraway suburb of Seattle, an acquaintance asked me about my research. When she heard the location of my dissertation research, she immediately responded, "Oh yeah, it's the Wild West out there." The phrase *Wild West* was invoked equally by Arizonans and non-Arizonans: it was shorthand for guns, lawlessness, Wyatt Earp, and the notorious shooting at the O.K. Corral.

In *Borderline Americans: Racial Division and Labor War in the Arizona Borderlands,* historian Katherine Benton-Cohen traces the history of the Arizona Territory and its borderlands. According to Benton-Cohen, the shooting at the O.K. Corral was "a battle over law, order, and border security that threatened a diplomatic emergency with Mexico."[12] The southeastern Arizona town of Tombstone boomed with venture capitalists, miners who left the California and Nevada gold mining camps and others who sought new wealth through the silver mines. During this time, the population of Tombstone was ethnically varied; most of its early residents hailed from places outside of the United States (not Mexico). Tombstone also attracted "desperadoes and outlaws" from other US territories, such as Montana, Texas, and Idaho, men who were called *cowboys*.[13] Unlike the original association of the cowboy as a ranch hand, these predominately white cowboys were a "lawless element that exists upon the border, who subsist by rapine plunder and highway robbery; and whose amusements are drunken orgies, and murder," and whose main victims were Mexicans.[14] The cowboys were suspected to have "purchased their liberty" by bribing a local county sheriff, Johnny Behan.[15] Suspicions of corruption dogged Behan and US marshals Virgil and Wyatt Earp. The Earps were gamblers and known brawlers, and Wyatt Earp's sidekick, Doc Holliday, was infamous and wanted for murder. Corruption, chaos, and violence were lasting characteristics of the frontier ethos of Arizona.

Benton-Cohen argues that the opposition between *cowboy* and *lawman* has its roots in regional and political differences. In this new post–Civil War era, the contest frequently mirrored the distinction between Democrats and Republicans, but even more importantly, it matched the division between those who did not desire the scrutiny of government and its regulations and those who welcomed governmental support.[16] Terror, wealth, and lawlessness flourished in Tombstone, but not because of a threat presented by Mexicans or their migration; instead, it was the violence perpetrated by the early Americans along the fault lines of political and regional distinctions that placed the town at risk. The notoriety of Arizona emerged again in 1899 when the then governor of Arizona, Nathan Murphy, petitioned for statehood in futility. When his efforts failed, he argued that "sectional prejudice, imaginary partisan policy, and pure selfishness" were the driving logic behind the denial of Arizona's inclusion into the union.[17] This lasting depiction of Arizona as a place of lawlessness, chaos, and delinquency laid the groundwork for the future rhetoric of crime to emerge.

Unsurprisingly, Sheriff Arpaio taps into these mythological narratives and explicitly applies them to contemporary principles of law enforcement. He explains his methods in his book, *America's Toughest Sheriff: How We Can Win the War against Crime.* In the chapter "Volunteers Unite," Arpaio charts out his logic for *volunteerism,* a regional practice in which citizens work in the capacity of deputized law enforcement. The volunteers, also known as the *posse,* are trained monthly in downtown Phoenix. Arpaio argues that the current incarnation of the posse is not a new idea; rather, he is drawing on the historically entrenched idea of volunteerism. He explains:

> The posse embodies something fundamental and necessary in the American Experience. It embodies Americans working and fighting and pledging their efforts and honor to the community. And no work, no fight, no pledge could be more deserving of effort and honor. . . . The posse is an old idea, born in the Old West, when the sheriff would deputize a band of local citizens to mount up and help him catch the crooks who had just robbed the stagecoach. I've adopted and updated the concept, making changes for the modern age.[18]

Although Arpaio draws upon the American myth of the Old West to contextualize his current methods of law enforcement, he is also informed by historical practices of US militarism. Arpaio defines himself as a career soldier; he has had a "lifetime in law enforcement" that started at the age of eighteen during the Korean War. During his sixty-year career, Arpaio has worked in law enforcement as a "beat cop," was recruited to the Bureau of Narcotics (now known as the Drug Enforcement Agency) in 1956, and in 1961 he continued his DEA tenure overseas in Turkey as part of the nascent drug war. Nearly fifteen years later, as part of the ongoing war against drugs, Arpaio was relocated to Phoenix. There he was given an assignment as the special agent in charge of Arizona. At that point, Arpaio's twenty-eight-year career was encapsulated in his fight against the "bad guys," those who benefited from Mexico's drug economy. From Arpaio's perspective, local posses, the war against drugs, and law enforcement are part of a larger framework of fighting crime, where illegal immigration is simply the beginning:

> Illegal immigration is the starting point of expanding criminal conspiracies, one rolling out into the next and into the next. That's why you need to understand (and it's really not too hard to understand) the link between illegal immigration and illegal drugs, and just how far the long malevolent tentacles of the [drug] cartels reach. The cartels are taking

Figure 7   Arpaio's War on Drugs. The cannon reads, "Blasting Away at Drugs."

over the routes for both businesses, and their increased opportunities to extract profit on both ends increases their power, as well as the suffering of every human being standing in their way.[19]

This passage illustrates how Arpaio's perceptions of crime and what he and his constituents call *illegal immigration* are based largely on certain historical and narrative patterns that stem from the mythologization of Arizona. The influence of outlaws and bandits amplified Arizona's image as a regressive territory where barbarism and lawlessness thrived. However, as Benton-Cohen observes, these associations were not always linked with people of Mexican descent. Current perspectives of Mexicans and Latinos as unrelenting lawbreakers and perpetrators of crime emerged during a crucial moment during state and national history when solidarity among workers and within labor movements was defined as anti-American. This moment of linking Mexican identity with anti-American sentiments crystallized during a strike by the International Workers of the World that resulted in the infamous Bisbee Deportation.

Mexicans, Anti-Americanism, and Labor Activism

In the early part of the twentieth century Mexicans living in California and Texas became increasingly associated with national anxieties about health, sanitation, and disease. In *Eugenic Nation,* historian Alexandra Stern links these concerns with eugenics research taking place at the turn of the twentieth century. The interest in eugenics was a public performance in nation-making and social engineering rooted in Anglo-American conceptions of morality. Stern connects the development of eugenics to entrenched colonial practices that emphasized the racial superiority of Anglo-Americans. The interest in eugenics stemmed from beliefs in Manifest Destiny that linked power, wealth, and genetic superiority to Anglo-American "stock." Stern maps the history of eugenics and links it to medical practices that focused on the US-Mexico border and issues of quarantine. Bodies of Mexican migrants were depicted as "contagions" and a "mestizo peril" that endangered "American seed stock."[20]

However, this depiction of Mexicans has not always existed in Arizona. After the US-Mexico War (known as "The American Intervention" in Mexico) officially ended in 1848, the United States had a stable, if tenuous, relationship with Mexico. Under the Treaty of Guadalupe Hidalgo, no territories were actually ceded; instead, the US-Mexico Border was established.[21] Mexicans living on the US side of the border were given the option of relocating back to Mexico or becoming US citizens. By 1876 when General Porfirio Díaz was elected as president of Mexico, the United States had fairly peaceful relations with Mexico due to Díaz's interest in financial and political stability. At that time, Mexicans were not the main targets of anti-immigrant sentiments in the West. In fact, Benton-Cohen points out that "the line between 'Mexican' and 'white American' was at first undefined, then inconsistent."[22] Rather, it was the Chinese who were labeled as the nation's "first 'illegal immigrants' and the first to be refused entry on the basis of nationality alone." The "Chinese inspectors," who were the forerunners of today's Border Patrol, targeted Chinese immigrants who came to the States via the US-Mexico Border. The phrase *Chinese wetbacks* was a pejorative used in some newspapers during that time; it "conjured an image of poverty, illegality, and racial otherness."[23] However, this perception drastically changed during the summer of 1917 and a series of strikes in Bisbee, Arizona, that were mobilized by the International Workers of the World (the Wobblies).

In the late 1800s, the newly developed copper mining town of Bisbee attracted people from a variety of backgrounds—especially immigrants. In response to the lawlessness and disorder of Tombstone, investors, mining companies, workers, and others began to demarcate social difference along the lines of race. Consequently, Bisbee became "a white man's camp," a place where workers from China, Mexico, and South America were excluded from the benefits regularly assigned to white workers.[24] Mexicans were able to live and work in Bisbee, albeit at a lower wage and at a different encampment—an area called the Warren District, which was designated for Mexican residence. This spatial separation underscored the differential wage system that divided Mexican from white workers; by the early 1890s, the pay of Mexican workers was less than half that of their white counterparts. According to Benton-Cohen the concept of the *American standard of living* and the differentiation of wages reinforced notions of race and masculinity in the Bisbee white man's camp. This monetary distinction amplified the effects on class differences that were ascribed to race. However, these normalized ideas would undergo serious scrutiny when Mexican union organizers eventually allied themselves with Anglo union leaders. The partnership of labor unionism and activism that reached across the racial divide turned out to be a significant threat to the social order in Bisbee, and it resulted in the mistrust of strikers, who were branded as anti-American.

Initially, Arizona had been a place hostile to union activity. Between 1906 and 1907, approximately 1,200 workers were fired for supporting a union. The Bisbee Industrial Association was staunchly pro-business and antiunion; they had a stranglehold on local politics in Arizona, because local business relied on investors and miners in order to survive.[25] However, by 1917 the ethnic composition among Bisbee workers had drastically changed. According to Benton-Cohen the Bisbee workforce contained "unprecedented numbers of Slavic, Finnish, and Mexican workers—the groups most likely to support unions and strikes."[26] Moreover, in 1916 the International Union of Mine, Mill, and Smelter Workers recruited 1,800 miners into their union, making it the first of the unions to have a noticeable presence. Meanwhile, the Industrial Workers of the World (IWW) was also gaining ground and gaining members in Arizona. One of their most successful strategies was to recruit minority members into their union, especially Mexicans. Union leaders understood that Mexican employees were the targets of discrimination; they were routinely funneled into surface work that did not command the higher salaries.[27] The alliance of Mexican workers and the IWW threatened to destabilize the power of the mining industrialists and their strategy of using ethnoracial stratification as a means to consolidate power.

However, the strength of the IWW was short-lived. Three months earlier, the United States had joined World War I. According to journalist John Fitch, the logic of wartime Arizona facilitated a rupture in the state that divided the citizenry into *good* and *bad* individuals.[28] This allowed citizens who were designated *good* to "break the law with impunity when dealing" with individuals perceived as *bad*. It was during this time that the stigma against IWW members as anti-American and as *American Bolshevists* began to emerge. James Byrkit, a labor historian, explains the predicament union members found themselves facing:

> The IWW bogey idea quickly spread and intensified. Reactionary business interests, eager to discredit any union, wanted the public to see an

image of the Wobbly as a lazy hobo whose philosophy was "sabotage" and the overthrow of capitalism. Whatever constructive qualities the IWW possessed, the press suppressed. Tales of IWW outrages gave newspaper readers a thrill. Sensational stories like that of the Everett Massacre in November 1916, reinforced the iniquitous reputation of the Wobblies, even though the IWW was cleared of blame. . . . With the coming of the war, logic was discarded and national excitement colored all issues. Little sympathy could be found for the IWW at the popular level.[29]

With the convergence of wartime national sentiment, growing anti-union rhetoric, and the desire for social order, the sheriff of Bisbee, Harry Wheeler, mobilized the Citizen's Protective League and the Workman's Loyalty League. These were vigilante groups organized to intercept the mobilizing activities of local strikers.[30] On July 11, Sheriff Wheeler began deputizing workers in the Loyalty League who were called upon the next day to arrest and detain nearly two thousand individuals, over 90 percent of whom were immigrants.[31] Approximately half of those arrested were of Mexican descent or from Eastern Europe. The question, "Are you an American, or are you not?"[32] expressed the reasoning behind national and local political activities: foreigners, individuals suspected of supporting the "overthrow of capitalism," and people perceived as a "threat" to the American nation were arrested, detained, and deported. During this time, immigrants, especially those of Mexican American descent, represented the antithesis of American identity.

The history of racial antagonisms in Arizona and the 1917 Bisbee Deportation demonstrate how social, geopolitical, and historical events intersect to produce the conditions necessary for militarization to emerge. For example, the processes of place-making and nation-building occurred through two main avenues: (1) the demarcation of work-related ethnoracial encampments (the white man's camp), and (2) the establishment of the US-Mexico border. They helped to redefine what it meant to be an American during the First World War. Consequently Arizona, as a recently incorporated state, became an epicenter for public spectacles of nationalist sentiment. Racial categories, labor practices, wartime loyalties, and place-making during the Bisbee Deportation combined to provide a public demonstration of nation-building and serve as a template for future demonstrations of national belonging, citizenship, and ethnic solidarity.

Borderline Identities: The Legacy of Cesar Chavez

The history of the Bisbee Deportation is embodied in the life and legacy of
the Mexican American labor leader and civil rights activist, Cesar Chavez.
Chavez is one of the most famous individuals representing the intersection
of union activism, civil rights, and the historical disenfranchisement of
minorities. His legacy inspires many events that occur among the activist
communities of Phoenix and Tucson. I frequently saw Chavez's photo, often
with Martin Luther King Jr., on numerous leaflets distributed throughout
migrant communities and during immigrants' rights protests.

Born in Yuma, Arizona, in 1927, Chavez came from a family whose
experiences mirror many of the troubles that migrant communities currently face. Chavez was exposed from childhood to systematic practices
based in discrimination and exploitation. During the Díaz dictatorship,
Chavez's family fled from Mexico to escape a life of financial servitude to
the infamous Terraza family. Although his family eventually owned a home
and small grocery business while he was a child, they lost both during the
Great Depression.[33] Chavez's parents were forced to move the family to
California, where they became migrant workers. While in seventh grade,
Chavez left school to become a full-time migrant worker. At seventeen, he
joined the Navy hoping to acquire skills that would benefit him later, but
quickly learned that Mexican Americans in the Navy were funneled into
manual labor jobs and unable to obtain marketable skills. After his two-
year tour, Chavez returned to migrant farm work for the next ten years.[34]

During the 1950s Chavez turned to work that focused on Latino civil
rights and joined the Community Service Organization (CSO). After
eventually becoming the national director for CSO, he left four years
later to start the National Farm Workers' Association with another community organizer, Dolores Huerta. During the 1960s and 1970s Chavez
spearheaded the workers' rights struggle among Mexican Americans in
California and Arizona. His successful activism with the National Farm
Workers' Association (later known as United Farm Workers) would be
the bulk of the rest of his life's work. His union was extremely influential;
it organized the Salad Bowl Strike, the largest farm strike in US history.
Lasting seven months, it led to enactment of the California Agricultural
Relations Act, a law that granted collective bargaining for farm workers.[35]

Chavez's legacy is mixed; whereas his critics view him as polarizing, his admirers continue to view him as a savior. He is described as both highly "charismatic" and a labor leader with numerous "shortcomings."[36] However, his record of nonviolence and protests based in spiritual fasting form the basis for the actions of current human rights activists and organizers in Arizona, and he continues to be a source of inspiration among immigrants' rights activists today.[37]

In 1993, when Chavez died in San Luis, Arizona, he left a legacy that shaped the conditions of possibility for Arizona to be the site of a national showdown on immigrants' rights. Chavez's own life history and position as a key figure in Mexican American civil rights activism illustrate how social, historical, and political conditions directly inform the lives of local residents and their agency. His life history and experiences offered him the remarkable ability to bring the injustices suffered by Mexican Americans into public view; his actions unquestionably affected the contemporary trends of activism in Arizona.

Conclusion

When we examine the history of Arizona as a US territory and as an incorporated state, we can see how the conditions of possibility emerged for contemporary practices of immigration and incarceration. With its long-standing image as the Wild West, a place notorious for its lawlessness and crime, Arizona later emerged as a state within a nation that was ready to prove its loyalty and its place in the Union. Thus, the question that Sheriff Wheeler posed to the individuals who were arrested—"Are you an American or are you not?"—is filled with layers of social and historical meaning. The question of *being an American* consolidated multiple social and historical threads that helped to construct categories of race, national solidarity, class differences, and antiunion sentiment. Today's debate on immigration echoes social and political conflicts that were generated during earlier periods of nation-building, but they are now focused on Latino migrants. The activities of Maricopa County sheriff Joseph Arpaio also draw on these historically derived narratives of crime, lawlessness, war, and the fear of perceived outsiders. Perhaps drawn to settle in Arizona by its prescription of Sunbelt Justice, residents favor punitive penal practices and mistrust perceived outsiders. Sunbelt Justice, along with the rise of the military-industrial complex, provided the conditions necessary to develop a constellation of social, political, and business strategies that focus on war, crime, immigration, and incarceration, targeting individuals of Latin-American ancestry.

The contemporary homeland-security-industrial complex is thus an example of how ideas interact and produce the conditions of possibility for the institutionalization of violence. These conditions rely on what the philosopher Ian Hacking describes as *dynamic nominalism*—the idea that individuals, based on their temporal location and history, are socially "made up," through processes of labeling and historicity.[38] This idea is especially appealing to me, because it is evident to me, after my time in the field, that current perspectives concerning immigration are the results of a dynamic process by which labels, categories, history, and geography converge. This nexus shapes how certain people are defined and come into being. Labels—such as *illegal, racist, border crosser, progressive, conservative, white,* and *Mexican*—assign particular values to individuals, and certain characteristics are ascribed to them.

Whether these characteristics are true is irrelevant. Instead, these labels are important anchors for people living in the community, because categorization helps them organize their world. This organization is part of a larger ecology that reinforces ways of being within a system. When individuals rely on particular categories to define their social world, they "change the space of possibilities for personhood."[39] Our categories influence how we understand the social world. The interaction of these categories has profound social, political, and material consequences, and I investigate this interaction in the remaining chapters.

Chapter 2
War Zones and the Work of the State

You know there's a war going on down here.
—*Eric, interviewee*

Phoenix, August 2010

On one hot evening in Phoenix, my adopted family got together for my belated birthday party. Everyone in the house was doing some kind of chore: Piper prepared food for the tacos, Renee prepared rice and beans, and Carlos ran to the local store to get wine. The chores seemed endless. Eric, a longtime activist in the group *Respeto!*, was setting the table for dinner, while Brian, a mutual friend of the family and of mine, organized chairs. I was a few feet away arranging some party decorations. There was light chatter in the room, mostly about party preparations. As usual, the discussion turned to immigrants, their rights, and unsurprisingly, *the border*. Eric listed the events of his day, which centered on activism. Suddenly he turned to Brian and said, "You know, there's a war going on here." Brian nodded furiously in agreement. I was not sure to which war he was referring—was it the *war on immigration* that people are accustomed to hearing about? The ongoing antagonisms between the two main political parties, which many interpret as *warlike*? Or something else? At first, I shrugged it off, thinking it was another one of the peculiarities of life in

Phoenix. Yet the ease with which friends and acquaintances used phrases such as *war zone* intrigued me. During my time in Phoenix, few days passed where someone in my immediate circle did not invoke the imagery of war.

When I asked individuals about their frequent use of war metaphors and imagery, I received mixed responses. Some people thought there was a real war going on in Phoenix, and others disagreed. In fact, some people did not realize they were using the language of war in their everyday conversations. However, every person with whom I spoke did agree on one aspect of the discussion: the constant *talk* of war in its various contexts affected the communities in which they lived.

One conversation I had with a participant demonstrates how individuals who are regularly exposed to the discourse of war interpret this language and incorporate it into their daily conversation. One of the few people who seemed wary of using the language of war was Kevin. He is a longtime volunteer with the group Ya Basta. Kevin works for a national aviation company and lives in an upscale suburban area. Over the course of two years, he spoke with me multiple times and used the war metaphor when discussing the subject of immigration. When I asked him about the use of the word *war* in everyday conversation, he made the following comment:

> You know it's funny that you ask me that question today. Just a few days ago, I sent an e-mail to a news reporter and asked her to please stop talking about the events out here and referring to it as a war. They like to sensationalize stuff, you know? It's not good for us, and it's not good for people to see that. It's different down here. . . . But it's not your typical war zone.

Once, within thirty seconds of sitting down for an interview at the local Applebee's in Tempe, Jimmy, an activist with Ya Basta, said, "Oh, we're in a war zone down here. There's no question about it." He proceeded to list the numerous ways by which he understood this. According to Jimmy, Phoenix was a "police state," there "were too many cops around" who only wanted to "racially profile innocent people." Exasperated, he blamed the "militiamen, vigilantes, racial profiling, leaving people for dead . . . the list goes on and on," as markers of a war zone.

What does this constant talk of war—literal for some, metaphorical for others—actually mean? In this chapter, I explore how the discourse of war and the use of the phrase *war zone* point to interviewees' concerns about national and local governmental failure. The discussion of war zones appears to be shorthand for the anxieties that emerge from deeply rooted suspicions of external meddling (or malign neglect) by the government, experiences of marginalization, and insecure livelihoods. According to my participants, these characteristics are all evidence of governmental and community breakdown.

Violence—in this case, *war zones*—is frequently perceived by analysts to be a symptom of a breakdown in the normal cultural, economic, or political processes of everyday life. According to this perspective, war is a failure of politics, or simply some destabilization in identity. Although this perspective has some use and is supported by numerous scholars, it fails to fully include the larger social and structural practices that inform the violence people experience in everyday life. Although scholars, such as Arjun Appadurai in *Fear of Small Numbers,* stress the tension between majorities and minorities, there are also a number of scholars[1] who argue that war is a kind of creation: it is a means of "making" the world that is specific to modernity. For example, anthropologist Glenn Bowman links violence to modernity. In his article "The Violence in Identity," Bowman observes that although "hurting" is an aspect of violence, it is only one aspect.[2] The production of violence helps to facilitate certain forces of transcendent creation and destruction that are necessary to "making the world."[3] According to some participants, the war that occurs in Arizona is "created" as a means to expand bureaucratic state power, although others consider it a necessary means of survival.

This chapter addresses two overarching themes related to the conceptualization of war among Phoenix residents: (1) war and its relationship to ongoing ethnic tensions and fragmented cultural identity, and (2) war as an instrument to expand bureaucratic state power, regulate populations, and repress awareness of class antagonisms.[4] Both of these are present simultaneously; war is both instrumental and operational. As I will demonstrate, the political and social environment of Arizona centers on the discourses of war and identity politics. The public fixation on war and ethnoracial identity obscures other phenomena that are taking place, such as the management of populations according to social and economic difference. On individual and collective levels, the performance of war—both literally and metaphorically—is a demonstration by citizens that illustrates the *failure* of the state to protect them. However, this expression of state failure is obscured through the activities of media pundits, activists, and ordinary citizens who habitually use the discourses of race and ethnicity to frame ineffective local and national governance. Any attempt to critique state power is immediately thwarted when individuals choose to ground critiques in the language of race.

In other words, the racialization of the immigration debate has resulted in a two-pronged effect: (1) in the short term, it has mobilized individuals along the lines of ethnicity, and (2) broadly speaking, the racialization of the immigration debate hides a grievance common to nearly all groups currently invested in the politics of immigration—that is, the exploitation and disenfranchisement of individuals, regardless of race or ethnicity. By framing the immigration debate in the discourse of race, activists and media pundits across the political spectrum unwittingly produce the labor needed to uphold statecraft. When individuals focus on racial differentiation, they ultimately conceal the social and economic factors that could possibly unite and compel them to work together. Instead, people continue to be *at war* with one another.

This chapter is largely informed by the work of George Lipsitz, a scholar working on whiteness.[5] I draw on Lipsitz to contextualize the discourse of war and to provide the reader with some insight into how this discourse intersects with notions of whiteness, identity politics, and class antagonisms. In *The Possessive Investment in Whiteness: How White People Profit from Identity Politics*, Lipsitz uses the term *possessive investment* to describe how "power, property, and the politics of race in our society continue to contain unacknowledged and unacceptable allegiances to white supremacy."[6] Lipsitz makes the argument that the triad of property, power, and politics has been dependent on and influenced by "the racialized history of the United States—by its legacy of slavery and segregation, of 'Indian' extermination and immigrant restriction, of conquest and colonialism."[7] His most salient arguments center on the notions of "law and order," immigration policy, and the connection between Anglo-American ethnic identity and war. Early on in his book, he argues that racialized agendas are not the property of one party over another; instead, both political sides are actually in favor of this possessive investment in whiteness. He explains:

Neither side has been required to make its arguments in explicit racial terms, but both have been able to carry out racialized agendas—the liberals under the name of respecting prevailing market prices, encouraging business investments in cities, and helping the "middle class," the conservatives under the guise of promoting states' rights, protecting private property, and shrinking the welfare state.[8]

One way this possessive investment works is through state governments' implementation of law and order policies, such as immigration. The legislation of Proposition 187 is an example of this. In 1994, the California electorate voted in favor of 187, a legislative measure "designed to deny medical treatment and to deliver excruciating pain and punishment to undocumented workers and their families."[9] Lipsitz argues that the enactment of legislation like Proposition 187 scapegoats minorities and becomes unnecessarily punitive:

> [Proposition 187] marked an important event in the contemporary reinscription of the possessive investment in whiteness. It not only unleashed an inflammatory and hate-filled wave of nativist anti-foreign scapegoating, but it also served as a key component in a campaign to insulate white voters and property owners from the ill effects of neoconservative economic policies. Blaming the state's fiscal woes on immigrants rather than taking responsibility for the ruinous effects of a decade and a half of irresponsible tax cuts for the wealthy coupled with disinvestment in education and infrastructure enabled the state's political leaders and wealthy citizens to divert attention away from their own failures. . . . The process of demonizing undocumented workers as "illegal aliens" emanated not from a respect for legality, but rather from efforts by executives from large corporations, small business owners, and individual employers to escape their own legal obligations and moral responsibilities to obey statutes mandating safe working conditions, a living wage, and dignified relations between employers and employees.[10]

In California, the possessive investment in whiteness is often fueled by conspiratorial fears by whites regarding "Mexicans" overtaking states such as California and the Southwest with language domination and plans to annex California to Mexico.[11] In his second term as governor, Pete Wilson ran his candidacy on this platform. As I explained in Chapter 1, Sheriff Arpaio uses a similar model and has repeatedly won elections over the past twenty years. One participant described Arpaio as notoriously "throwing the book" at illegal immigrants. Although activists have tried repeatedly over the years to evict him from office and even attempted a recall referendum, these attempts have failed. In the 2012 election, he won more than 50 percent of the votes to be reelected as Maricopa County sheriff.[12] During my time in Arizona, all humanitarian activists expressed dismay over the sheriff's political strategies. However, Emilio, a participant who recently left the activist community after many years, expressed his frustration with activists whom he labeled as "distracted." He observed that constantly "going after Arpaio" was a waste of time:

> You know what? What these people do isn't activism. What they do is protest politics. These activists are fair-weather activists. They go out and protest for the fame, for the glory, for going after Arpaio so they can be on the news, be in the papers. I've been telling them for years that protest politics is not the same as activism, helping people with their daily problems. Who is going to help the migrants when they can't go outside to work? Or need to go to the store? Or pick up their kids from day care? Protest politics is just stroking people's ego, bringing them fame. That's why I don't do anything with these activists anymore. They just go to their comfortable homes after the protest is over and don't do much of anything else. They're distracted and they waste my time. I'm sick of them. I'm starting to organize networks of people that are willing to help migrants so they won't have to expose themselves to the police, have friends go to the store for them, things like that. What is going on in their daily lives is more important than going after Arpaio.

Emilio refers to protest politics in Phoenix as a *distraction*. But a distraction from what? According to Lipsitz, the politics of immigration represents "conspiratorial fears" of white individuals that reinforce a possessive investment in whiteness. This investment not only "secures the benefits of past and present discrimination in perpetuity for affluent white voters," it also simultaneously deflects "the anger of downwardly mobile whites toward the exploited immigrant workers upon whom the lifestyles of the rich depend."[13]

Lipsitz's explanation is useful, but an explanation that relies on an analysis of whiteness has its limits. This kind of framework reinscribes categories of race in an environment already polarized by this discourse. Many people of Euro-American ancestry have few avenues to express their own experiences of human suffering, alienation, and growing sense of insecurity or downward mobility. One participant explained her interpretation of the situation with the observation that "people unconsciously adopt whatever language is around them and they just include it in their daily life without thinking about it much." This participant points to the fact that people rely on language practices that are already part of the discursive landscape, and they do so without necessarily being aware of the consequences.

So as Emilio points out, most humanitarian activists do "miss the point" and fail to acknowledge that underneath the guise of protest politics, there are class-related disparities. He highlights this with the complaint that "They go to their comfortable homes after the protest is over and don't do much of anything else." After Emilio noticed this within his own activist community, he subsequently began to develop plans that were more relevant to the actual lives of people belonging to migrant communities.[14]

The following cases illustrate that the discourse of race and fixation on identity politics train individuals to "miss the point." Although the issue of racism is presented as part of a humanitarian agenda, phrases such as *white people* or *racists* trivialize the difficult experiences of lower-middle-class and working-class whites. Because discussions of class antagonisms are subsumed under the category of racial antagonisms, individuals who experience discrimination via class differences are unable to express their experiences of disenfranchisement except through the vocabulary of ethnoracial categories. This helps to reinforce the depiction of whites as racist. It further polarizes any extant discussions and amplifies an already volatile social and political environment and allows the conditions for violence to erupt.

Unconscious Expressions—Class Antagonisms, Identity, and War

On a fairly warm Sunday morning in May 2009, I attended a "Walk for Peace and Dignity" in downtown Phoenix. This protest focused on the rights of undocumented individuals and, as they self-describe, peoples "indigenous to the North American region." The five-mile walk started at the central downtown area of Phoenix and ended at the Maricopa County Jail. At the jail there was a counter protest—a group of individuals who seemed to be affiliated with an ultranationalist group. Some people waved the confederate flag; others were dressed in neo-Nazi uniforms. One man gave the "Heil Hitler" salute. Another protester held up a sign that read, "Go back to Mexico, take your swine flu with you!" He appeared to be physically agitated and wore a surgical mask. People shouting "Fuck you" littered the soundscape. In the sweltering heat of Arizona, not only was the land dried up and emitting a menacing heat, the people seemed to be just as hot and irritable.

The advocates for the rights of border crossers heckled the nativist counter-protesters. As I stood uneasily near the police line that divided the two groups, two women next to me shouted across the police lines: "You lazy ass motherfuckers. We clean up your shit. We wipe your babies'

Figure 8   Anti–illegal immigration protesters. Phoenix, May 2009.

asses. You're too fucking fat and lazy to clean up after yourself. So, fuck you." A few feet away I heard,

> "You dumb ass. Fucking racist."
> "No you're a racist. You hate your own kind. You hate white people. And look at you—you're white, hating white people. You're pathetic."
> "Fuck you. So what if I am white. You're a racist asshole. Dumb white trash. Fuck you."
> "No, fuck you."

In these exchanges, the discourse of race intersects with the local politics of Arizona. But a fault line emerges later, one that is based in class differentiation. The first incident included two young women of Latina descent who emphasized economic differences between the two ethnic groups. They also pointed to a deficiency in the work ethic of the Anglo-American counter-protesters, criticizing them as *fat* and *lazy* and shouting, "We clean up your shit." The second incident occurred between two Anglo-American men who hurled insults at each other, accused each other of being racist, exchanged racial epithets, and antagonized and egged each other on. Each incident expressed an implicit component of social differentiation and antagonisms rooted in class, but expressed in racial terms.

Why "Racist"?

The dominant trope in the immigration debate is racism and the depiction of those who support border enforcement as *racists*. However, Arjun Appadurai points to a more nuanced understanding of the divisiveness entrenched in the politics of immigration. In *Fear of Small Numbers,* he argues that since 2001, the global increase in sectarian violence has centered on what he describes as the "anxiety of incompleteness."[15] This is a feeling of social and economic insecurity that has recently increased with the forces of globalization. Appadurai explains that populations who are native to a region and once considered the majority have, in fact, become minorities in recent times due to their ever-decreasing "small numbers." It is the tension between minorities and majorities that often results in ethnonationalism and ethnocidal tendencies. Appadurai observes that

Numerical majorities can become predatory and ethnocidal with regard to small numbers precisely when some minorities (and their small numbers) remind these majorities of the small gap which lies between their condition as majorities and the horizon of an unsullied national whole, a pure and untainted national ethnos. This sense of incompleteness can drive majorities into paroxysms of violence against minorities.[16]

The convergence of majority/minority differences with the "forces of globalization" further exacerbates and fuels "large-scale social uncertainty." As a result, this becomes the breeding ground for genocide.[17] "Large-scale social uncertainty" and the desire for security are concerns that arose in a conversation I had over dinner with some friends of mine, Leslie and Allen. At the time, Allen was unemployed; he had previously worked as a supervisor in a local immigration detention center. Leslie, a homemaker, spent her days in community-based activities. Both Leslie and Allen express concern with what they perceive as an influx of undocumented individuals into the United States. In this conversation, Leslie expresses frustration over being labeled a racist because of her position in favor of the US-Mexico border wall:

Leslie: Why is this racist—to be for the border fence? To want people to come here legally? I don't understand. You don't invite a burglar into your home if they are breaking in. If they break in you, you call the cops, right? Also, why is it that if we don't like Obama we are racists? That actress—Janeane Garofalo—she said that if we don't like Obama, then we are racists! That makes me so angry. That is so unfair. They're constantly calling us racists. You know, I didn't make up my mind that I didn't like you based on your last name. I didn't call you bad names or anything. You are here and you are welcome in my house. The liberals—they just want to call everyone racists to make us look bad. I don't trust Obama's policies, not because he is black, but because he lacks experience. He was a junior senator—

Allen (interjecting): With no governing experience.

Leslie: And why can't we see his birth certificate? If he is born here, then why not? Just be open with information. If they are not open with information, then how can we trust them? And I saw it—I saw it in the newspaper. There was a sign at one of those pro-immigrant protests. . . .

It said, "Give us free housing, free food, free health care—give it to us free or we will keep killing cops!" How can they do that? Why aren't they arrested? That is a death threat, they should be arrested. How can they do that?

Here, Leslie challenges the stereotypes of Republicans and Conservatives that are circulated by pundits and entertainers. She understands that the oversimplified arguments usually touted by political entertainers are "unfair," and points to me as an example of her openness toward ethnic difference. Leslie seemed to be highly aware of how she, as a "conservative" middle-class white female, was portrayed in the media. One night while Allen was reading the newspaper, Leslie and I watched a rerun of *CSI*—a show I had never gotten around to watching. We eventually began talking about immigration. Leslie further expressed her frustration with the label of *racist*:

> *Leslie:* When our friend told us you were coming to visit and you needed a place to stay, I saw that your last name was *Torres*. I welcomed you into my home. I didn't make any assumptions about you or where you were from. I mean, I figured that maybe you were Hispanic or something, but that didn't matter to me. It's not race that matters, it's what's inside. And it really makes me angry that people keep calling us—people who want the border enforced—that we are racists. I'm not. I welcome all the new neighbors into the neighborhood. There's the Vietnamese couple upstairs, they're new. I baked them cookies. And I'm always concerned about the Mexican family with the girl and the little dog. She's so cute. I think they left [Ciudad] Juarez and came over here because it was too much going on over there. I think she's in school.
>
> *Nicole:* Do you know if they are documented?
>
> *Leslie* (shaking her head): I don't know. And I don't ask.
>
> *Allen* (chiming in): But if I did find out they were here illegally, I would have to report them.
>
> *Leslie* (nods her head): Yeah.

In this example, we can see Leslie critique the use of the term *racist*. She complains it is often misused or abused. Although there clearly are racial tensions in Arizona, the vocabulary of race occludes the larger context of actions and events that surround the issue of immigration. Whereas Allen seems more focused on law and order, Leslie explains that when a person is labeled as a *racist,* it becomes an ad hominem attack; it is an easy way to discredit what the person is saying. She suggests that the use of these labels becomes a simple way to undermine forms of intellectual or political difference. Leslie understands that she is caught in a discursive trap. This trap is what critical theorist Terry Eagleton describes as *semiotic closure*—the support of dominant ideas through the exclusion and denigration of those that are heterodox.[18] As a result, polarized situations emerge, the possibility of dispassionate engagement disappears, and divergent views are silenced.

I had a similar experience in an e-mail correspondence with Jodie. Jodie is an activist who refers to himself as an "anti–illegal immigration activist." He describes a similar dilemma. Refusing an interview, in an e-mail to me he explained,

> We no longer grant interviews to academia, which is far too biased and untrustworthy, and to the media. The media is beholden to businesses that pay for advertising and hire the illegal workers, which is a felony and 100 percent preventable.
>
> Illegal immigration is about money, not people. It is an unfair exploitation of taxpayer funds. An unfunded mandate from big business and corrupt governments (Mexico and the United States). Where is the compassion for the citizen taxpayer here??? Where is their representation??? Their protection??? Citizen taxpayers never achieve special interest status. . . . It has nothing to do with race. Playing the race card is a tactic to intimidate detractors from speaking up, and it works, mostly. Do you really think ICE and border patrol do racial profiling … no one else is either. We support their efforts, does that make us racists? Insane.
>
> Have a beef about illegal immigration? Then people will overgeneralize about why, and they won't assume in your favor either, no benefit of the doubt, they won't be cutting anyone any slack out of the goodness of their heart. . . .
>
> And it is anti–illegal immigration, not anti-immigrant, which is another common trick bag, these are distinctions that make a big difference
>
> Hypersensitivity about the race issue altogether, you can pin the tail on any donkey you like, but nevertheless, it is the pink elephant in the room that everyone can see but are unwilling to acknowledge. . . .

> Again, there is no national council of the white race, but there is the national council of la raza ... members state that la raza means community or family, but I'm not buying it. It [La Raza] is ethnocentric, which is PC, but not for everyone, which is very convenient politically wouldn't you say? The blade only cuts one way, that's what makes this issue so hard to debate.

Jodie explains the double-bind for those in favor of the border wall: according to liberal/progressive politics, one cannot be in favor of the border wall without being labeled a racist when he says, "People use the race card, not because it is the truth, but because it works." Jodie echoes Leslie's frustration with the tendency of pro-immigration/humanitarian activists to equate people in favor of border enforcement with racists.

The subject of race and racists pervaded nearly every discussion of immigration I encountered in the field. In contrast to the conversations that I've described so far, immigrants' rights activists insisted that individuals who approved of border enforcement were "really racists in hiding." In most conversations, interviewees observed how the repeated use of racialized language might even set the stage for the normalization of violence against Latino migrants and that there was no other way to talk about immigration. Moreover, many people remarked on how, once the discussion is thus framed, the rhetoric of anti-immigration policy (or anti–*illegal* immigration policy) is intractable. For example, Paulo, a local immigration rights activist, shouted,

> What's an immigrant? Do you know? What does the "im" mean? "Not." It means "not." Not a migrant. We're not migrants? We've always been migrants. We've been moving back and forth for centuries. They just up and decided one day that the land was theirs. And now they call us immigrants. We've always been here. They're just calling us something else.

Felix, an attorney, reinforced this idea. He linked it to derogatory metaphors that he thought were used to portray the local migrant community. In the following quote, Felix describes the technique of using language and vivid images as a means to integrate hostility toward migrants into the daily lives of Phoenix residents:

Figure 9   Flying saucer constructed by immigrants' rights activists with the phrase "We Are Human." Phoenix, May 2009.

It's a *hate foreigners* environment. A bunch of hate groups moved down here in the last few years. It's like a gift handed to the anti-immigration folks. The thing we're fighting against is people who have the ability to

Figure 10   Anti–illegal immigration activists. Phoenix, May 2009.

mainstream their hate. They keep using words like *occupation, invasion, epidemic, illegal, alien, war*.

These same themes had already emerged during my first visit to Arizona. In December 2008, I spent a weekend with some close relatives of mine, Sara and George, who live in a suburb of Phoenix, along with their teenage son, Jacob, who was seventeen. Sara and George are an interracial couple; they moved from New York City in 2002 to the Phoenix area for the milder weather, peaceful surroundings, and cheaper rent. While cleaning up dishes one night, they started asking me about my dissertation research. When I explained my interest in local perceptions of immigration, Sara waved her hand and shook her head.

Sara: Really, Nicole, there are too many of them here.

Nicole: Too many of who?

Sara: You know, immigrants. Mexicans are everywhere. We have to stop the bleeding.

Nicole: Bleeding?

Sara: Yes, the bleeding. They're bleeding us dry. The schools, the hospitals . . .

George: They're coming here illegally. Lemme ask you a question. If someone broke into your house, what would you do? You'd call the police right?

Jacob (in the living room): Oh, God, here we go again . . .

George: You'd call the police, right? They're breaking into our home. They need to get out.

Nicole: But you emigrated, Sara. You're from Panama. How is that different?

Sara: The illegals—they're taking jobs away from us, using our hospitals, our schools. It's too much. I am struggling here trying to make ends meet. They can't just run over the border because it's there. It's not right. I came here the right way.

Nicole: Have you had any difficulty finding a job because of illegal immigrants?

Sara: No.

Nicole: Have you had any difficulty getting service at a hospital because of illegal immigrants? Or has Jacob had any problems at school because of illegal immigrants?

Sara: No. But I see where you're going with this. We're not racists, you know.

George (agitated): They're breaking in. [*Pointing to the door.*] They need to get out!

The conversation with Sara and George exemplifies the themes I repeatedly heard while interviewing people in favor of the border wall. Sara stressed the economic component by using the analogy of a bleeding body with immigrants akin to an injury (or parasite) draining the body of its life force. George, on the other hand, adopted the language of criminality. He likened border crossers to criminals guilty of "breaking and entering." Over the course of a few days he repeatedly interrogated me with the argument, "If someone broke into your house, what would

Figure 11   Anti–illegal immigration protesters. May 2009.

you do? You'd call the police, kick 'em out. They're breaking into our home. They need to get out."

The tensions exhibited in these interactions are not manifestations of recent policies or the result of the incidents of September 11, 2001. Instead, conversations like these are deeply rooted historical patterns and social and spatial habits, as I described in the previous chapter.[19] One afternoon over a cup of coffee, Kevin (an activist with Ya Basta), whom I introduced earlier, reflected on what he viewed as some of the general characteristics of people who move to Arizona:

> I don't know, the folks here are weird. You've got the people who were born and raised here and their families have been here for generations. Then you've got the people here who move here, like me, looking for a change, something new. That's also why I got into activism. I didn't plan on this, it just happened, you know? The things people do here are so ridiculous that it made me want to protest. But then there's a lot of people down here that don't want to be bothered with anyone, anything.

Figure 12   Anti–illegal immigration protesters. Phoenix, May 2009.

They just want to be left alone and live in their houses. Behind their walls. Shut the door on other people's problems, you know what I mean?

Kevin's reasons for relocation to Arizona are similar to those of Sara and George. Sara and George left the East Coast looking for better weather and a better life, fleeing from the stress and strain of city life. Arizona seemed to be the perfect place to "get away" from the city—a place with plenty of sun, clean streets, and, at the time, cheaper housing. Sara's sister, Maria, who still lives on the East Coast, shared her own perspective on Sara's predicament:

Sara, she's always running from something. First she said it was the [drug dealers] in the city. Then she said it's because the city is so dirty. Blah, Blah, Blah. But drugs and dirt are everywhere. And so are people that you don't like. If she keeps it up, she'll be running for the rest of her life. Who's going to be there for Sara if something happens? Suppose someone gets sick? There's no one in Arizona to help her there. She had a heart attack once already, and there was no one there to help her and her family. Being out there all alone is dangerous. That stress and strain of being alone can kill a person. . . . Ay!

Maria links the desire to escape with the experience of encountering difference. A longtime resident of New York City, she views Sara's desire to escape as an aversion to difference, especially when she comments, "But drugs and dirt are everywhere. And so are people that you don't like." This is similar to Kevin's statement that people who move to Arizona do so to isolate themselves, or as Kevin says, "to be left alone in their houses. Behind their walls." The desire for walls, and for isolation and protection, reflects the social and economic processes that have been part of Arizona's cultural landscape for more than four decades.[20]

As we saw earlier in this chapter, the political landscape of Arizona is distinguished by public sentiments (as expressed by Sara and George) that gravitate toward isolationism and the criminalization of people perceived as *other*. As I explained in Chapter 1, Mona Lynch's chronicle of Arizona policy and practices helps to contextualize how the conditions of possibility emerge for individuals, such as Sara, Eric, and the anti–illegal immigration activist Jodie, to rationalize their actions. This is a political ethos marked by individualism, a frontier mentality, and mistrust of the government and of outsiders.[21] Consequently, the perceptions and treatment of immigrants, as well as the border enforcement policies, have been deeply influenced by these ideologies. These ideologies are central to how people understand and order the world in which they live.

Sara, Eric, and Jodie all rely on their membership in the nation-state to explain their antipathy for migrants. For them, the nation-state serves as a symbolic ordering of space and time, one that does not recognize the contested history of Arizona as a territory or, originally, as a part of Mexico. Geographer David Harvey offers a perspective for understanding the ideological stakes implicit in the conversations that I had with Sara and George. He argues that political constructs, such as the nation-state, are "symbolic orderings of space and time ... [that] provide a framework for experience through which we learn who or what we are in society."[22]

If we apply Harvey's analysis of the postmodern compression of space and time (that is, space contains compressed time)[23] to the border politics and social practices of immigration, the logic of participants becomes clear.

The social and political landscape of Arizona is a site where the identities of people, their uses of space, and existential meanings are continuously contested and recreated. Harvey explains, "value and meaning are not inherent in any spatial order ... but must be invoked. The idea that there is some 'universal' language of space, a semiotics of space independent of practical activities, and historically situated actors, has to be rejected."[24] For residents like Sara, Eric, and Jodie, the social and political demarcation of the border erases the history of centuries of migration and destabilizes the legitimacy of historical practices of migration. This spatial organization is enforced by invoking the language of crime, as in the use of the words *illegals, criminals,* and *citizen.*

The Work of the State—the Missing Vocabulary of Class

The comments of Leslie, Allen, Sara, George, and Jodie each point to underlying themes of social differentiation according to race, local class antagonisms, and a desire for law and order. These three themes, although often decoupled, are actually interconnected. Sara and Jodie each made arguments about financial struggles. Both were acutely aware that their positions on immigration produced an expected knee-jerk response of others who labeled them as racist. However, neither Sara nor Jodie ever mention class differences. In fact, why would they? Part of the American ethos and ideology is that the United States is classless; there has been little, if any, discussion of class differentiation in the past fifty years.[25] As Lynch points out, the political ethos of Arizona is deeply embedded in individualism and the rights of "citizens." This sentiment is primarily expressed through residents' support of border enforcement and protection.

In the United States, social relationships are informed by a deep history of class antagonisms and practices of racialization—phenomena that emerged from the racialized policies and practices of Anglo-American identity in the antebellum period. In *The Wages of Whiteness: Race and the Making of the American Working Class,* historian David Roediger argues that "whiteness was a way in which white workers responded to a fear of dependency on wage labor and to the necessities of capitalist work discipline."[26] In other words, the social construction of whiteness is directly influenced by the dependency of lower-class whites on their affluent white counterparts. This tension crystallized around the ever-increasing social importance of wealth, the dismantling of the Confederate states, and the newly found freedom of African Americans. The recently emancipated African Americans became concrete evidence that economic and social capital was about to be drastically redistributed, which whites, particularly in the Southern states, perceived as a threat. Impoverished lower-class whites found themselves scrambling to reconfigure for themselves a newly constructed identity of whiteness and independence. According to Roediger, the American Revolution created certain conditions of possibility—in this case "it would help create an America in which many more working freemen would be tempted to define themselves against slaves"—that is, along the lines of social and economic difference through the process of racialization.

The opposition between *free, independent, and white* versus *slavery, dependence, and blackness* gradually emerged after the Civil War and Reconstruction. Here, a fault line began to emerge, delineating social and economic differentiation. Pejorative terms for lower-class Anglo-Americans, such as *white trash,* appeared. *White trash* became a *stigmatype,* a "stigmatizing boundary term that classified unacceptable and acceptable identities … and create[d] categories of status and prestige."[27] Thus *white trash* is a term used to stigmatize whites who fail to achieve the social standards that allow them access to the normalized category of whiteness. Thus, terms such as *trailer trash* and *white trash* depict a state of unfreedom, lack of education, squalor, and dependency.

One of the few interviewees who expressed any identification with supporters of the border wall was Eric, the activist I mentioned at the beginning of this chapter. Eric expressed his understanding of the difficulties that both he and other citizens (white and nonwhite) experience, including lack of opportunities and devastating unemployment:

> I really came down here to do work in geology. I didn't expect to be unemployed like this. I mean it's been years. There's nothing to do down here. No money, nothing. People are angry and frustrated. The other day I was standing out here in the heat, dead noon. I was asking myself, "What the hell am I doing out here?" It's hot as hell, the heat is exhausting. People scream profanity at me from their car. Sometimes I'm the only one out here. I want to live, okay, have a good job. But there is

nothing out here. I didn't expect this for myself. But I'm here; it gives me something to do. Because you gotta do something out here. Something has got to give you meaning. Because just doing nothing will make you angry, drive you crazy. . . .

The anti-immigrant people, I hate to say it, but I understand them. I understand why they are so angry. You try to make a living, you try to put food on the table for your kids and stuff. But the government, they're screwing everyone; they don't care. Everyone is screwed here. No jobs. Some of these white people here, they have no education, no jobs, no health care. And they're citizens. I understand why they are angry. And my situation—I'm a lot like them. But you can't let yourself go there. It's just not right. But still—I ask myself what the hell am I doing out here because this place, this place is crazy. It's going to kill us all. And that's why I'm out here, I guess. Because you gotta do something. I gotta keep going. They can't take away my humanity from me, you know?

Here Eric observes that "Some of these white people here, they have no education, no jobs, no health care"; and he understands "why they are angry." Eric recognizes the class discrimination that downwardly mobile Anglo-Americans experience, indirectly describing what Lipsitz calls "the possessive investment in whiteness." However, Eric is also aware that individuals who are legal citizens of the United States are rightfully angry. They have "tried to make a living" and failed, and yet the government does not care. Eric also identifies risk factors for violence when he observes "doing nothing will make you angry, drive you crazy." He sees that people who have "no money, nothing" are experiencing downward mobility and become emotionally and mentally vulnerable.

White working-class people who are alienated, frustrated, and economically struggling may choose ultranationalist behaviors to articulate an "anxiety of incompleteness" in the only way that is currently available—by using the language of nationalism and citizenship. This social differentiation is organized along the lines of class but expressed in racial terms; it allows little, if any, room for downwardly mobile white citizens to publicly express any legitimate frustration with their plight. The double bind creates social conditions that fortify isolation and alienation. In its most severe forms, this dilemma manifests in the social world as extreme nationalism and militarism. Drawing upon the work of Hannah Arendt, Lipsitz makes a similar observation:

putatively democratic societies become ready for totalitarianism when loneliness becomes a routine feature of everyday existence. The combined effects of deindustrialization, economic restructuring, and the oppressive materialism of a market society where things have more value than people feed a sense of isolation and loneliness. . . . Militarism becomes one of the few spaces in such a society where a shared sense of purpose, connection to others, and unselfish motivation have a legitimate place.[28]

Thus, militarism and nationalism become fields of expression for individuals who are denied the language of class to describe their dilemma. However, Lipsitz appears to minimize the consequences of repressing class differences. When class differences are stifled, the deleterious effects of militarism and nationalism are amplified. Individuals become vulnerable to extreme forms of nationalism where, as one participant described it, "people have nowhere left to go."

Conclusion

In this chapter I have explained how, although somewhat useful in the proximal future, racialized discourses of immigration ultimately reinscribe racial tensions; this reinscription cultivates a social environment where violence is more likely to erupt. Scholars, such as Lipsitz, use racial conflict as an explanation for nation-building, but they do not explicitly identify racial conflict as a form of statecraft. According to my participants, however, there is a synergy that occurs among nationalism, identity, and war. This interaction is a maneuver of statecraft; it is a mechanism of the state used to manage and regulate populations and it diverts attention away from class antagonisms and economic insecurity. This is a key feature of American statecraft, and it relies on the enactment of patriotism, border activism, vigilantism, and associated citizen action groups to provide a sense of belonging. These affiliations subsume class antagonisms and divert attention to racialized discussions of immigration and ethnic exclusion. In this ideologically charged setting, individuals become initiated and trained to do the work of the state. By being blind to the problems that are located in class differences—yet expressed in patriotism, nationalist sentiments, and phenotypical differences—ordinary citizens are "mobilized" as soldiers in the immigration debate to reinforce existing social and political divisions.[29] This political sleight of hand is crucial to the process of statecraft; I explore this further in the next chapter.

※

CHAPTER 3

CAPTIVITIES AND CONTAINMENTS

THE TENSIONS OF CONTROL

Another day in Marikafka County.
—Jeffrey, during an interview

August 2010—Immigration Court, Phoenix Arizona

"Well now, would you look at that!" exclaimed the judge to the court clerk. He shook his head in disbelief. "See here, I denied this person residency, and the head office overturned my decision about deportation. They wrote back saying they are allowing this person to stay because they have 'extenuating circumstances.' Extenuating circumstances! There was nothing extenuating about them." He sighed, shook his head in futility, and shifted the case file to a stack of files on his right side. In the room was an assortment of individuals busy with activity: a Spanish translator, several defense attorneys, a lone state attorney, numerous clients who were classified as unauthorized or out-of-status immigrants, and a host of family members and friends whose ages ranged from toddler to grandparent. They seated themselves in the front of the courtroom and waited anxiously to hear their family members' cases. While everyone settled in, the judge and the court clerk continued to prepare for the day's activities.

This scene was part of my first visit to the immigration court in Phoenix. That first day, I arrived fairly early in the morning, and while walking into the courthouse, I saw that the building was small and nondescript; it was oddly dwarfed by the oversized parking lot surrounding the two-story building. When I entered the building, I noticed three things: the surveillance cameras, the simplicity of the building, and the vending machine on the lobby floor. It seemed to be so dead that I wondered if I was even in the right place. I ventured up to the second floor, where I walked up a small, open-air, shallow flight of stairs. To my left was a door. A security guard stood there, smiling at me. He asked, "Hey, how are you doing? You here about a client?" I explained to him what I was doing, and he replied, "Oh, yeah—sure. Trials are not open to the public, unless you have permission; but you can go to as many master's hearings as you want. Those are always open to the public."

Master hearings are scheduling conferences attended by a group of people who have been charged with a crime. They are generally quick meetings between client, judge, and attorney—if the client even has one (some individuals represent themselves)—mostly designed to schedule future proceedings and organize what needs to be done. These are not cases to decide the fate of the defendant; rather, they are administrative meetings to decide on how to proceed. A person attending his or her first master hearing (there is often more than one) pleads to the charges and tells the judge what forms of relief they wish to seek—such as asylum. The hearings are usually quick and seem to be efficient; the goal is to rapidly move cases and people. Each hearing lasts little more than five to seven minutes. The judge sets a time for submission of the defendant's documents and schedules the next hearing date on the master calendar, which may be another master or an *individual hearing*. The individual hearing is what most people recognize as a trial.

The primary objective of the master hearings is to schedule dates for future cases. Numbers, names, and a brief description of case and client situations are provided at each client hearing. During my visit in August 2010, the judge and the attorneys scheduled court cases for May and August of the following year and as far into the future as January 2013. I wondered, where are these out-of-status people going in the meantime? I asked the security officer this question at the end of the day. Shrugging, he explained:

They go home … it's kind of like an honor system. Not everyone goes to jail. That's crazy. Most people are out and about. They have kind of like a probation officer, but it's an ICE officer. They check in with the ICE officer about once a week, keep their current address where they live up to date, and they go about their business. . . . They go back to work, they go back to their boyfriends, girlfriends, parents, whatever. We can't keep everyone in jail. There's too many people. Most of Phoenix would be in here! So, the people mostly who are just here trying to work and aren't committing any criminal offenses are released with a probation officer. That's all we can really do. It's mostly the criminal offenses that we wind up jailing. Or, they get the ankle bracelets or something like that. It's crazy. [*Shrugs again.*] That's life.

For some reason, my observations at court reminded me of rearranging a stack of books—there is effort, yet the number of books remains the same. The officer's comments also pointed me to the fact that individuals, regardless of their position on immigration, expressed concern about the lack of competence of the US government. He also pointed to the disorganization inherent within the immigration system, something that many participants also recognized. For example, as we saw in the previous chapter, Sara complained that the city and the nation were "bleeding." The language she used conjured images of an injured body, no longer in balance and being drained of life. The theme of control came up regularly. I frequently heard phrases such as "the government has lost control," "the government has no control," and "we're [the United States] losing control."

This led me to wonder: When and how does the state implement mechanisms of control? Although a number of scholars agree that there is an increase in the normalization and routinization of populations, scholars diverge in their perspectives. Some address the role of the state and its connection to various expanding mechanisms of control. Others argue that the state's connection to what seem to be ever-expanding control mechanisms causes them to question whether or not control is even the purpose.

In this chapter, I focus on two aspects of governance that originate from social and bureaucratic practices that rely on a logic of surveillance and detention. This process results in the social, psychological, and physical misery of targeted individuals. There are two main scholars who inform my approach. I draw upon the work of Jonathan Simon, a legal scholar whose work explores the effects of the expansion of governmental control.[1] Simon uses the expression *governing through crime* to refer to the use of political and juridical rhetoric that centers on threats and risks posed to citizens by outsiders. When law enforcement and government officials use the rhetoric of crime control, they are able to provide citizens with the appearance of limiting risk and providing them with security. I then turn to the work of Ruth Wilson Gilmore, which focuses on how individuals are captured in the bureaucratic system of detention and manufactured as unproductive subjects of the state. They are "incapacitated" and designated as unworthy. Consequently, these individuals are subject to the harsher aspects of society that are derivatives of governing through crime. *Incapacitation* results in the systematization of places, policies, and objects to create a unique security apparatus, known to critics as the *homeland-security-industrial complex.*

The homeland-security-industrial complex is actually a constellation of policies and practices that transform disenfranchised individuals into unproductive and criminal subjects. For the remainder of this chapter, I explore the ways in which governing through crime and incapacitation reveal how the role of the state affects whether or not an individual is able to participate as a *citizen-consumer.* When individuals fail to maintain their status as citizen-consumers, they are classified as *unproductive subjects* of the state. In other words, they are criminalized. Depending on a person's position within neoliberal practices of governance, the state's role can either contract or expand. However, the intensity with which people are being constructed as unproductive subjects results in procedures that many participants argue infringe on their civil liberties, such as excessive surveillance and racial profiling. For the remainder of this chapter, I explore these consequences.

The Factory

During one of my visits to immigration court, I witnessed a deportation trial. The defendant was an undocumented man from Romania who had entered the United States via Mexico. He had left Romania more than two years before and stayed for some time in Mexico with the goal of coming to the United States. On the day of my visit, he was requesting political asylum. The defendant explained that the Romanian police were corrupt and repeatedly tried to extort money from him and his family. He and his family used to have property in Romania. However, he was not sure of the status or condition of the property—either it was still there and abandoned or confiscated by corrupt police officers. The defendant's case seemed to be weak. He was unable to convince the judge that he fled his country for political reasons. Meanwhile, his attorney seemed exhausted, disorganized, and preoccupied. I saw little, if any, actual advocacy from her on behalf of her client. Everyone looked tired and weary.

This moment seemed surreal: people were adhering to the rules of court, and the rules either did not apply or were close to meaningless. The defendant told a less than credible story of why he wanted to stay, and the judge yawned and rolled his eyes. The defendant's attorney was ineffective, and the state's attorney sat there and casually checked off another box for deportation. Little effort seemed required, and the entire scenario appeared to be routine. Nearly four hours later, after finding out the judge had decided to deny him asylum, the defendant would be scheduled for deportation. I left the courtroom feeling drained. Relieved to be able to stretch my legs, I caught a glimpse of the security officer whom I had met earlier that day. He nodded at me and smiled.

> *Nicole:* Wow, that trial was long.
>
> *Officer:* Boring, too, right? [*He shook his head and shrugged.*] Those trials are long and boring. Sometimes I think the judges may be nodding off. Those trials are ridiculous. Everyone in there is bored. Even the defendants.
>
> *Nicole:* Hey, that attorney—what was up with that? She didn't seem to try to defend her client.
>
> *Officer* (shaking his head in futility): Man. . . . She don't even try. People come in here and tell me she is the worst attorney to have. She is unprepared, lazy. She's just a warm body. In it for the money. [*He rubbed his fingers together.*] Come back again tomorrow for the master hearings. I'll get you in. It's at 10 a.m.

The officer points to the tedious quality and impersonality that are characteristic of the immigration trial process. He alludes to the monotony that the employees of the court system experience along with its desensitizing effects when he acknowledges that the defendant's attorney was "in it for the money." The next day, one of the local activists, Eric, came to the courthouse with me to observe and keep me company. After a few minutes, his eyes widened. He exclaimed, "Look at this, it's just like a factory, moving people around—a revolving door of jailing people, like cattle." While Eric reflected on the inhumanity of it all, I reflected on the system that I began to view as a *contraption*. Contrary to public perception, Immigration and Customs Enforcement (ICE) was *not* jailing everyone—as the officer said, that was impossible. As he explained earlier, there are far too many people for the state to keep track of; immigration court merely gives the appearance of enforcement. But with dates for follow-up court dates as far out as 2014, I wondered, what does this mean? Everyone I spoke with seemed to know there are out-of-status workers and undocumented migrants. It seems to be a fact of life for Arizonans who work with it, around it, or against it. Thus, although publicly decried, immigration is also an understood part of the social life. The tension between chaos and control was embedded in the landscape, and the theatrics related to it appeared both essential and commonplace. However, as I mentioned earlier, public sentiments concerning migrancy and immigration frequently manifest through popular notions of citizenship. This is especially evident in how the sheriff and police departments use crime to govern the neighborhoods and social networks throughout Phoenix.

Governing through Crime: Citizens and Criminals

Although migration is part of the social and historical landscape of Arizona, the tensions between migrant communities and law enforcement are the result of the dominant social and political imaginings of the nation-state. The social realities of the borderlands areas straddle multiple social and cultural histories. These histories include the experiences of indigenous people who have lived in the borderlands for centuries, such as the Tohono O'odham, the mestizo populations found in both countries, and more recently, the histories of the currently recognized nation-states—the United States and Mexico. To strengthen this political distinction, law

enforcement officers (such as Sheriff Arpaio), politicians, border enforcement supporters, and others attempt to reinforce notions of citizenship
and freedom by policing the boundary between who is a citizen and who
is not. This distinction is a mechanism by which individuals understand
and adapt to socially constructed notions of freedom. For example, in
Powers of Freedom: Reframing Political Thought, British political scientist
Nikolas Rose outlines a dialectical process that underpins present-day
conceptualizations of freedom. He argues that the way citizens understand
the notion of freedom is not by simply defining what it means to be *free*.[2]
Instead, contemporary practices of governance and social imaginings of
freedom are defined by highly illiberal practices, such as incarceration and
a citizenry adapted to everyday constructions of criminality that define the
boundaries of a socially acceptable self. As with governing through crime,
freedom and security are highly shaped by their antitheses—captivity and
precariousness. Where individuals feel they belong and how they perceive
others within these categories are what make governing through crime
effective; all individuals are subjects and objects of surveillance.[3]

Rose argues that individuals who do not (or are unable to) participate
in an entrepreneurial ethos are "failed citizens" or "anti-citizens," people
who cannot live up to their expected role of citizen-consumer. Thus, by
default, the state exiles individuals who are disruptive to state, business,
social, and community interests. These failed citizens and anti-citizens
are subsequently sorted into categories of social exile, such as criminal or
homeless.[4] The understandings formed around who is constructed as a
criminal are known as the *crime complex*, an assemblage of principles and
discursive practices that produce a habituated sense of danger from others.[5]

For example, Piper, a woman I interviewed, reported her experiences
with Claudio, a young man from Argentina. Claudio lacked documentation
and as a result was *illegal*. Claudio wanted to find a job and earn a living in
the United States, but he was terrified of being arrested. In the following
excerpt, Piper explains the dangers of being classified as an *illegal alien*:

> You know Claudio, right? When we first met him, he didn't have his
> papers and he hardly spoke a lick of English. He's not even Mexican;
> he's from Argentina. That goes to show that everyone who comes up
> here is not Mexican, but hey, you know how that goes. But anyway, he

spoke no English, poor guy; he was like a little baby. He was working for some crazy woman, cleaning her pool and stuff like that. But when she didn't feel like having him around anymore, she just dumped him on our doorstep, with the clothes on his back and a frozen chicken. A frozen chicken! Just like that. Crazy! I couldn't believe it! I mean what the fuck? A frozen chicken? Like he's a piece of property? A pet? ... Claudio stayed on our couch for months. No complaints. We fed him; he helped around the house with stuff. And he watched English television all the time he was here. He would sit on the couch and force himself to watch and learn. And with all that TV, his English is great. He was a fast learner for sure. I'm just happy he learned English. He has a little job now and everything. He still doesn't have any papers, he's definitely afraid to go outside because of all the immigration craziness here, being arrested and all ... but he's learned a lot.

Piper indirectly indicates that Claudio lacked not only the language skills, but also the financial means, to self-govern and be free. In the eyes of many local residents, Claudio was a criminal. He lacked money, did not have a stable social network, and was "unproductive." Terrified of being arrested, the only job Claudio could find resulted in his relegation to a slave-like status—or as Piper observed, "a piece of property." Based on this logic, Claudio is undeserving of the treatment given to *legal* human beings and became subject to exploitation. "Dumped" on her doorstep, he lived in sequestration for nearly a year.

Claudio's situation illustrates the conflation of illegality and criminality, a merger that conditions individuals to become subjects of self-inflicted practices of surveillance. Claudio understood the danger of being undocumented. He understood the likelihood of being watched by others, and because of this, he was afraid to go outside. Eventually, Claudio's situation turned out quite well; he had a small, but protective network. For others, however, the situation is quite grim. In the absence of the most basic support system, the role of the state in their life expands.

Thus, the social construction of criminals conveys to citizens their role in the state.[6] It requires that individuals are habitually exposed to binary constructions, such as *legal versus illegal* and *criminal versus citizen,* and internalize their meanings. This is a technology of governance that individuals consciously and unconsciously rely on to regulate their lives and shape their behavior. However, these dichotomies do not neatly map onto the actual conditions of Arizona. For many Arizonans who are of mixed ethnic identity, especially Mexican Americans, the categories of legal/illegal and criminal/citizen are exercises in racial profiling.

Governing through Crime: "Crimethink" and "Crimespeak"

As I explained earlier, governing through crime expands the power of the state by helping to shape what people think of as essential attributes of a safe and secure community. However, a consequence of this form of governance is that its effects become magnified in unforeseen ways. For example, governing through crime amplifies what some view as the racial profiling of minorities; many of my participants, especially the humanitarian activists, felt that the heightened level of racial profiling endangered their friends, families, and themselves. In *Golden Gulag,* Gilmore identifies how the amplification process works. Drawing upon the work of James Ferguson, she explains that the discourse of crime within the United States is a mechanism to capture and contain individuals, describing this process as *antidevelopment.*[7] Because Gilmore models her discussion of antidevelopment after Ferguson's description of the discourse of development, it is worth quoting him here. He describes the *discourse of development* as

> a distinctive style of reasoning, implicitly (and perhaps unconsciously) reasoning backward from the necessary conclusions—more "development" projects are needed—to the premises required to generate those conclusions. In this respect, it is not only "devspeak" that is at issue, but "devthink" as well.[8]

Gilmore's analysis points to a rationale that is essential to governing through crime. It operates as a kind of implicit understanding that relies on a discourse of safety—and is operationalized through the language of crime. In other words, whether to incarcerate a population is not the question. Instead, the questions are, *Where should we contain individuals? Which groups?* These questions reveal the rationality of *crimespeak* and *crimethink.* Crimespeak and crimethink are the mental and psychological constructs needed to produce the conditions for the capturing and warehousing of individuals. It is through the built environment and material culture that prisons, jails, and detention centers gradually become routine backdrops of the local landscape.

The consequences of governing through crime are illustrated in the experiences of an activist friend of mine, Carlos. One morning, while out driving around Phoenix, he took me downtown to show me the Maricopa County Jail. He made a point of taking me past the trucks so I could capture a photo. He exclaimed in frustration, "See! Did you see those trucks? That's some bullshit right there. How can this NOT be racist? There's some crazy shit going on in this town." Later in the interview, Carlos complained, "I was born and raised here. I've been stopped two times by the police. Why? Because I look Mexican. My crime is DWB—Driving While Brown. It's bullshit."

For Carlos, the terms *illegal immigrant* and *illegal immigration* are forms of crimespeak that mark individuals who have chosen to enter the United States without proper documentation or outside of legal channels. This is an

Figure 13   Arrest. South Tucson, January 2011.

example of what Ian Hacking identifies as a *looping effect,* normative patterns of thinking and social habits that result in the dynamic of thinking and habit "egging each other on."⁹ The construction of *illegals* feeds into a particular kind of *crimethink* that manifests itself in the activity of racial profiling. Crimespeak connects to *crimethink,* because individuals who are visibly *other* and predominately Latino, become the victims of racial profiling, even though undocumented individuals arrive in the United States from a variety of countries. However, *crimespeak* (the discussion of illegal immigration) and *crimethink* (the practice of looking for a visible other) operate under the aegis of Anglo-American nationalism, and their use results in charges of racial profiling from targeted communities who are perceived as ethnically other. Because this discussion is so polarized, any attempts to unpack the complex, racialized logic that informs such thinking is often thwarted. Instead, conversations that center on the complexities of racial profiling devolve into hackneyed discussions of racism, a trajectory that seems to end conversations, not expand them.

Figure 14   Truck with poster calling for help against illegal immigration and trafficking. Phoenix, December 2008.

Figure 15   Sign on the Fourth Avenue Jail in Phoenix, Arizona.

Illegal immigration is a foundational idea essential for governing through crime in Arizona. It is a system of political and juridical practices that targets individuals who are ethnically other and perceived as security risks. Discursive and rhetorical strategies, such as the use of the term *illegal alien* and analogies (as in the story of Sara and George) of *breaking and entering*, invoke deviancy and criminality and habituate residents to socially constructing others as criminals. These terms emerge as social and mental habits that enter mainstream conversation, becoming normalized terms that help the formulation of criminality to emerge in a given environment. Governing through crime sets the stage and the framework by which subjects can and cannot choose possible fields of action, and it limits the possibilities of political being for individuals in places such as Phoenix, because there are only citizens and only criminals. Consequently, discussions of racism divert attention away from how individuals gradually adapt to processes of governing through crime, processes that reduce their agency while also increasing activities of militarization.

From the general public's perspective, crime may seem to be a neutral topic, and this impression benefits government officials and politicians from both

Figure 16   Graffiti in Central Phoenix.

sides of the political spectrum. They rarely, if ever, question whether there is an actual increase in crime. Instead, they portray themselves as *tough on crime*. Thus, governing through crime, which appears as necessary and apolitical "has been the point of insertion for a bureaucratic state power." However, this kind of governance is "neither benign nor universal in its application."[10] When government officials construct crime as a priori and commonplace, they are able to "whisk away the political realities" that have dire consequences for disenfranchised individuals, their families, and their communities, and it results in what many participants describe as a *police state*. Ruth Wilson describes this process as *incapacitation,* or the warehousing of surplus, unwanted individuals.

Governing through Crime: "Doing Nothing" and "Incapacitation"

> It's a disgrace here. I'm ashamed of this. It's like when
> the Berlin Wall came down, this wall started to go up.
> —*Officer Sanchez*

I met Officer Sanchez on a tour of a borderland Detention Center in December 2010. An older woman in perhaps her late fifties or sixties, she was assigned to escort me around the ICE and Border Patrol facilities during my two-day tour. A petite woman who seemed to take everything in stride, she was not only helpful in answering my questions, but she also radiated warmth. Officer Sanchez took pride in doing her job, yet she also was firm about enforcing the border. I imagined that her presence was to dispel the stereotype that numerous humanitarian activists reported: Immigration and Customs Enforcement was a "cruel and racist institution." My goal was to get an idea of what the facilities actually do and how they implemented strategies of capturing and detaining individuals. As it turned out, Officer Sanchez was the public presentation—as one of the other staff members described, the "public relations face"—of Immigration and Customs Enforcement.

When I asked Officer Sanchez why she worked at the detention center, she said, "It's a good job; it pays the bills." Officer Sanchez was in administration for the detention center. She spent the morning with me and gave me a tour of the facilities: the mess hall, living quarters, small library facilities, intake area, medical facilities, social workers area, yard and recreation area, and—most surprisingly—the adjacent courtroom facilities. The courtroom was actually on the site of the detention center. The Processing and Detention Center is a large and sprawling facility conjoined with Border Patrol—two distinct entities that were components of the larger complex of Immigration and Customs Enforcement. I was only allowed to tour the detention center; I learned later that any tour of the Border Patrol facilities would require a separate visit.

This detention center visit and multiple trips to Mexico constantly reminded me of the border's porosity. I recalled that, although the US government seems to assert control over the US-Mexico borders, in many instances, it does not have control. As I saw in the Phoenix immigration court, there may be some control, but detention centers and border walls are fundamentally cosmetic devices; they act to conceal the social and political porosity of the adjoining countries. Nowhere did I see this more evident than in the on-site court facilities at the Processing and Detention Center. Although some detainees were physically present for their court hearings and proceedings, others "attended" their hearings via closed-circuit television from places as far away as New Mexico. When I asked Officer Sanchez why this was so, she explained that it was due to the "shortage of both court-rooms and judges to hear all the cases." Later on, during a conversation over lunch, Officer Sanchez lamented the conditions of living in a border town:

> You know, it's terrible down here. The sad part about this is that a lot of us, we have family that lives across the border. I have a sick aunt that I haven't seen in years because the border violence is so terrible. And I'm worried about her health, too. We used to just come and go as we please, but we can't do it any longer. The violence has gotten so bad—we would be risking our lives if we go over there. It would be nice to see our families, go back and forth like we used to, but not anymore. The cartel violence is so bad ... we're all stuck here ... [*She drifted off and shook her head.*]

Officer Sanchez hints at an important point: the pervasive sense of being stuck or trapped. As Piper explained, the emphasis on crime results in deleterious effects both for *citizens,* such as Officer Sanchez, and for perceived *criminals,* such as Claudio. This lack of movement, a feeling of being stuck or trapped—either physically, psychologically, or both—is a theme I explore next.

Governing through Crime: Detention Centers and Incapacitation

During my visit, some officers stressed that the detention center was not a *prison,* that the Processing Center was a *detention center,* used for holding people until their deportation date. However, the structure of the facilities and everything about its layout had the look and feel of a prison. The mess hall, the sally ports, surveillance cameras, barbed wire, and the detainees' uniforms were echoes of the jails and prisons I had visited or worked in previously. Functionally, it was a prison—but for extranational individuals. There seemed to be disagreement among the workers at the detention center concerning its purpose. Officer Sanchez and two social workers debated the use of the phrase *detention center* versus the word *prison*:

> *Social Worker 1:* People waste away in these prisons. They are prisons. They like to call them detainees. But they are treated like prisoners.

They have no freedom here. People come here looking good, and after they've been here for a while, they get broken down by the system. Their color starts to change. They just get hunched over. They start looking scared and lifeless. A lot of these people just want to go home. They get depressed here and they start wasting away. Some people go crazy. It's really sad. Sure, they made a bad decision. Now they are separated from their families and loved ones. But they just want to go home now. I don't know why we have to keep them here. Just send them back. A lot of them just want to go back.

Officer Sanchez: But a lot of them don't either. Some want to stay. Like there was that one guy who kept fighting and fighting to stay. He tried to use the law library here to get out of every scheduled deportation. We eventually sent him back.

Social Worker 2: Yeah, but a lot of them want to go home. It's sad. I mean why do we have to keep them here in limbo like this? Why? Why? They are just wasting away here. It's so sad. It makes me want to cry.

This conversation between Officer Sanchez and the social workers points to the ambiguity surrounding the function of the detention center. Although the term *detention center* indicates a place that is meant to detain individuals for short periods of time, individuals are often left there indefinitely. Indefinite detention takes a toll on prisoners, who suffer from social and psychological incapacitation. In the next section, Allen, whom we met in Chapter 2, critiques both the efficacy of the detention center and its effects on its detainees.

"Reducing the Badness"

About three years earlier, Leslie and Allen decided to relocate to the borderlands for Allen's work. Allen has an extensive history of working in corrections and for the federal government. In the following conversation, he expresses how the prison system (including detention centers) needs to be completely overhauled:

Allen: My job is to reduce the badness. Places like these, they're bad for people in general. It's terrible to be in there. Why do we need to make it any worse?

Figure 17   Outside of a detention center, December 2010.

That place is dysfunctional, just like all these other places. There's tons of administration there. What are they doing there? Just moving one piece of paper over to that pile over there. It's the same every day. They just come there and collect their check while people are wasting away—and they don't care.

Nicole: But they say the turnover is usually about two weeks.

Allen (shaking his head): More like two years. People go crazy here. This place is not fit for humans! And make no mistake—these places are prisons, even if they call them detention centers. People waste away in here—away from their families, their friends! Sure they broke the law, they did something wrong. Just send them back. Why are we holding people up in here? It's criminal. They [Immigration and Customs Enforcement] are in the business of doing nothing . . . nobody cares. Nobody cares how long these detainees are here. Nobody cares, and nobody knows what this place is supposed to be doing.

Suddenly Allen gets up, goes into his bedroom, and pulls out a letter he received from a man who was caught gambling in the United States on an expired tourist visa. Rather than immediately deporting the man and his wife (in fact, they both had plans to go back to their country of origin, because they had children there), ICE detained the couple indefinitely. For two years they were ensnared in the long, serpentine process of deportation. Allen threw his hands up in the air and explained:

> That guy, Chem, he was such a nice guy. I hope he's doing okay now. There was no reason for him to be in prison for so long. They should have just sent him back immediately. But, no, they kept him in detention; he got really depressed, was crying and stopped eating because he was worried about his family and kids. Why? Why? I helped him get out of that mess. It took me a long time, but I got on those guys' cases. Look here, here is the letter he sent me thanking me for helping him return to his country.

> Dear Mr. Allen:
>
>   I send you a very hearty welcome; the sound begins from deep within the bowels of one's lungs/soul to signify the depths of one's joyous feeling at being alive. You may not know how humbling it is to feel when someone like you goes out of your way to help someone in distress given your already busy schedules. It is very appreciated and we can never thank you enough for interceding on our behalf. So many months away from our children is a nightmare both ways and you've contributed immensely to curtailing it.
>
>   We extend to you and your lucky blessed family our life-long invitation to visit us anytime, Sir. No matter how long it takes, we will patiently await over the horizon for your arrival and whoever you bring with you. Till then, our good friend, please take care and stay safe.
>
>   May our Almighty Heavenly Father continue to bless you, your family, and all that are dear to you abundantly always.
>
> Always your friends,
> Chem and Lina

After handing me the letter Allen sighed, sat down in his easy chair, and turned up the volume on Fox News. There is a news story on federal "wasteful spending," including the much maligned study of "cow burps." Pointing at the television with his remote, Allen exclaims, "Now look here! Our government is spending money to study cow burps. *Cow burps!* With a government like this, how can we actually *do* anything?"

Allen's observations point to an important problem that officers, social workers, mental health counselors, volunteers, and other employees in the detention center acknowledged: the Kafkaesque state of indeterminate suspension that detainees encounter. This state of suspension is what Gilmore describes as *warehousing*. Drawing upon the history of California, she argues that the prison boom that took place there was an integral part of "urban and rural political and economic restructuring." During a time when the state experienced a persistent economic crisis, prisons became a geographic and economic solution for specific kinds of "surplus" racialized people, land, places, and even certain kinds of capital that were labeled as *idle*, a "problem."[11] People and places were categorized as "doing nothing"—*unproductive*. From this perspective, human beings became objectified as *problems* that need to be solved. Through social and economic disenfranchisement, these problematic populations were funneled for containment within prisons.

Likewise in Arizona, warehousing becomes a catchall solution to the euphemistically labeled *immigration problem*. Gilmore's notion of warehousing applies to out-of-status immigrants and border crossers. Similar to the families described in Gilmore's book, the migrants who are detained now belong to a category of people whose "entire way of life has been made surplus." These individuals, regularly depicted as idle, a drain on economic resources, breeders, and unsanitary, are considered to be a social and moral problem that needs to be contained. Unauthorized migrants who are arrested become part of the surplus or *idle* populations that Gilmore identifies. The grinding poverty and the structural inequalities that disenfranchised individuals experience prevent them from being recognized as members of the state. Instead, they are funneled into the prison system where "entire ways of life" are designated as surplus and unfixable.[12]

Conclusion

The social landscape of Arizona reveals a tension between the classifications of legal and illegal that shapes and informs communities. This condition is addressed locally through practices rooted in the logic of governing through crime and the detention of unwanted individuals. The logic that underpins governing through crime is depoliticized and assists in the recruitment of individuals to participate in the surveillance of individuals whom they suspect are illegal immigrants.

These social and political practices discipline and regulate citizens. Rose's notion of *failed citizens,* or *anti-citizens,* is crucial to understanding how the dialectical process embedded in governing through crime operates: it is a vast network of political and juridical practices that relies on the social construction of a criminal/citizen binary logic that participants view as oppressive. Gilmore's analysis of the role of the state is vital to understanding the consequences of this logic. According to Gilmore, entire communities and populations are captured and contained in both the literal and metaphorical sense. Undocumented individuals, such as Claudio, who lack the requisite capital to participate fully in the neoliberal market, have no place within the United States. They are in danger of being classified as *idle,* a surplus population on which an "institutional apparatus is unleashed" to capture, contain, and exclude.[13] By looking at both of these perspectives on the role of the state, we have a clearer view of when and how the role of the state shifts, expands, and contracts in the management of populations. More importantly, these practices point to systemic issues that many participants acknowledge: citizens and noncitizens alike live in a climate that is increasingly volatile—socially, economically, and politically. This condition results in existential and psychological despair. However, many such economically strapped citizens, who expect protection from the state, are rapidly undergoing a sense of economic and political insecurity that they usually identify with *illegal aliens.* I explore this predicament in the next chapter.

CHAPTER 4
DIAGNOSING THE BORDERLINE

Borderline (def.): n. A boundary separating two
countries or areas. A division between two distinct
or opposite things: the borderline between ritual and
custom. adj. Only just acceptable in quality or as
belonging to a category: references may be requested in
borderline cases.[1]

. . . to grapple with the borderline concept is to
wander onto a battlefield littered with the remains of
earlier definitions, fought over by bitterly contending
factions, and shelled by other factions who would
obliterate the concept altogether.[2]

On the morning of the Tucson shooting, I interviewed Dan one last time. I
sat in the kitchen of his idyllic B&B and reflected on my previous conversations with him. During each of my visits to Tucson, Dan had complained
about the effects of the border wall on his neighborhood and on Tucson
in general. He felt that the border wall does not promote safety; rather,
the wall exacerbates divisive thinking and behavior. He stressed the need
for border communities and for the nation as a whole to engage in what
he described as "holistic thinking":

Everybody wants good health, to be safe, and have adequate food. If we legalize drugs, wouldn't that make everyone safer? It drives down the price, drives down illegal trading; drugs wouldn't be such a big deal. We can't keep one side of the border safe without trying to keep the other side safe. The border creates that "us against them" mentality. And it is constructed like that—to create war, to put people in prison—things like that. All this emphasis on lines and borders ... borders recreate Republicans versus Democrats, Christians versus Muslims ... it makes it hard to solve problems.

In this comment, Dan clearly explains that the border wall "creates that *us against them mentality*" and makes it "hard to solve problems." In other words, having a physical marker isn't promoting conditions of safety; instead, the wall helps to cultivate environments that are actually unsafe.

I started this account with the events that occurred during the Tucson shooting, and I return to them in this chapter. They point to a paradox that many participants acknowledge: Despite an emphasis on safety and security, especially concerning the danger represented by *illegal immigrants,* some of the most notable acts of violence originate with individuals who are, in fact, citizens of the United States. At least three major incidents of multiple murders have occurred since my dissertation research began in 2009—one of them being the case of Jared Loughner and the notorious Tucson shooting.

Unsurprisingly, in the case of Jared Loughner, one of the immediate (and predictable) responses was to question the sanity and the responsibility of the individual committing the violent act.[3] The example of Jared Loughner followed the usual media pattern: the shooter was "crazed," "insane," and "evil." Yet, why Arizona? Why are individuals, such as Loughner, and (as we will see shortly) vigilantes, such as Shawna Forde, drawn to such polarized environments? This is the basis of the question that I posed in the beginning of my introduction: *What kinds of environments help to assemble the conditions where violence is possible?*

In this chapter I examine the social context of three Arizona residents who are depicted in local or national media as *crazy* and/or *evil.*[4] Each individual assigned a certain social and political meaning to the US-Mexico border. As mentioned in an earlier chapter, numerous scholars have written about the purpose of the border, and specifically of the border as a project of statecraft.[5] In this context, the border can be said to function as a cosmetic device; it is a tool of *impression management* that enhances and reinforces the image of a unified nation-state.[6] However, in this chapter I examine the US-Mexico border as a social artifact *and* as a metaphor for the production of certain social and psychological conditions that are identifiable as diagnostically *borderline* on both individual and collective levels. Here, I draw upon the work of scholars inside and outside of anthropology to explore how individuals who are invested in the protection of the border wall enact internal and external conflicts that resemble the behaviors of individuals who have been diagnosed with borderline personality disorder (BPD). Many of the attributes and behaviors exhibited by a person diagnosed with BPD are similar to the collective attributes and behaviors I encountered in a variety of people while conducting my fieldwork in Arizona.

Thus, for the purposes of this chapter, I am using the diagnostic category of *borderline* as an explanatory device and a conceptual tool. Both scholars and media commentators have paid a great deal of attention to the superficial characteristics that are assigned to the politics of immigration and its rhetoric. This results in a presentation of Arizona as a caricature of "crazy people" and, as one person commented, "a place full of rednecks, racists, and Republicans." One late night talk-show host used Arizona as the basis for a scornful joke, calling Arizona "the meth lab of democracy." With this emphasis on the politics of immigration and racism, there has been little, if any, academic analysis dedicated to understanding the fundamental social and psychological conditions that compose the geography and the discourse of Arizona politics. Instead, the media depictions of Arizona and its residents are often stigmatizing; they invalidate the vexing experiences of people who live there. This is where I turn to psychologist Marsha Linehan's analysis of BPD to provide a theoretical framework for discussion; in the first part of this chapter, I present a basic summary of Linehan's conceptualization of dialectical failure. I then go on to provide ethnographic examples that illustrate how dialectical failures are exhibited in the social world.

Borderlines and "Dialectical Failure"

I was first exposed to Linehan's work on dialectical behavior therapy about four years ago, a little before I started my dissertation research.

At the time, I was an intern at the Monroe Correctional Center–Special Offenders Unit (SOU) in Monroe, Washington, where I was assigned to do basic counseling and talk therapy with the inmates, all men. I was also to help with SOU *programming* by teaching classes in life skills to men who were scheduled for release within the next six months. Every inmate in the unit was diagnosed with a mental illness; at one point, my supervisor told me that there were a "bunch of guys in the unit who [were] kind of borderline" and that Linehan's book, *Cognitive Behavioral Treatment of Borderline Personality Disorder,* was a "must have." He was right; the tools Linehan offers in her book were invaluable. I found myself able to connect with "difficult" inmates who were torn and conflicted about their predicaments. Eventually, in a few surprising cases, a few admitted to past experiences they had not shared with anyone else in the unit.

I have chosen to use Linehan's assessment of borderline personality disorder because she offers an analysis of why patients diagnosed with a borderline condition are so difficult to treat. Observers frequently stereotype a person with a borderline syndrome as *manipulative* or *devious.* Linehan argues that these terms are pejorative and may prevent therapists (and others) from being able to care for borderline patients:

> However it seems to me that such pejorative terms do not themselves increase compassion, understanding, and a caring attitude for borderline patients. Instead, for many therapists such terms create emotional distance from and anger at borderline individuals.[7]

Similar to patients diagnosed with BPD, events in Arizona are particularly difficult to understand: like the physical landscape, the social climate is harsh and volatile, producing an atmosphere where highly reactive behavior and conflict are routine. As I spent time talking with participants, attending protests, observing the landscape, and paying attention to media portrayals of Arizona, I noticed that the social and political climate of Phoenix reminded me of the time I spent working with the inmates and of Linehan's work regarding *dialectical failure.* The social and political discourse in Phoenix was filled with vitriol; from my perspective, any possibility of improvement seemed to be at a standstill. I witnessed name-calling among participants, ongoing mistrust, verbal and physical fighting at protests, and routine expressions of hostility. The personal and collective experiences of being divided, feelings of isolation, and experiences of alienation matched Linehan's description of borderline patients and the predicament of dialectical failure. Her model is useful for understanding an environment, like southwestern Arizona, that is fraught with conflict and is physically located near a borderline.

The term *dialectics* has its origins in the Greek language. According to the Oxford English Dictionary, the word *dialectic* has its roots in the word *discourse,* meaning, a "running to and fro."[8] This oscillating, back and forth process is also evident in the philosophical ideas of Marx and Engels, where dialectical materialism is defined as a conflict of social forces produced by material and economic conditions. A similar *struggle,* or *war*, occurs on the geographic terrain of the self—both the body and the psyche.[9] Linehan synthesizes Marxian and Buddhist concepts into a holistic approach that uses the notion of dialectics as a means to understand internal conflict. Linehan describes three basic characteristics of a dialectical approach:

1. *Interrelatedness and Wholeness*: As described similarly in the work of Gregory Bateson[10] and others,[11] a dialectical worldview acknowledges a systems approach to the world, where everything is part of a greater whole. Thus, as Linehan points out, "identity is relational"; it can only make sense in a larger social ecology. Linehan observes, "It is the whole that determines the boundaries."[12]

2. *The Principle of Polarity*: The social world is not static. Likewise, Linehan specifically states that "reality is not static" and is constructed of internal opposing forces that are in a continuous state of tension.[13] When these opposing forces have the opportunity to integrate, synthesis and change become possible.

3. *The Principle of Continuous Change*: In a dialectical model where opposition and synthesis are natural processes and are encouraged, one recognizes that change is a logical consequence of this continuous process of the dialectic. If we are able to understand this fundamental tenet, capacities for growth, illumination, and healthy change emerge. A person or group that holds a dialectical worldview acknowledges that internal oppositions exist and that by integrating those oppositions, change is possible.

For decades cultural anthropologists have stressed this very same point: the social world is dynamic and in a state of continuous change. In spite of this understanding, a dialectical model is seldom applied within anthropology. One critique of using this model is that it undermines the goals of smaller groups that tend to rely on fixed notions of self and identity (such as ethnic groups) in order to promote solidarity and preservation of tradition. Although there is some truth in this, there is a real benefit in understanding the context in which oppositional structures of identity emerge (such as legal/illegal and pro-/anti-immigration). A dialectical worldview helps us to see the function in dysfunction and seeing this can help us recognize and understand the sources of polarization found in everyday conversations.

I do not assume that the participants in this chapter were or could be diagnosed with borderline personality disorder. Instead, by using the diagnosis of BPD as a metaphor and the information available on three case studies, I attempt to describe the social and political dynamics of this region as part of an organizing system that suffers from, as one participant described it, a *rupture*. This rupture is the result of a dialectical failure, and the collective behavior found among individuals who live in this area resembles the symptoms of an organism at war with itself. I refer to this condition as a *borderline existence*. In the following section, I describe the characteristics of dialectical failure. Later, I demonstrate how this condition emerges in the borderlands of Arizona.

Dialectical Failure

1. *Social Splitting*: A dichotomous worldview, or rigid practice of dualistic thinking, is what psychologists describe as *social splitting*. This *either-or* model of the world leaves little—if any—room for complexity, ambiguity, and fluidity in everyday life. Through this oppositional logic, persons are continually sorted into competing camps. A similar pattern of splitting exists in the borderlands regions of Arizona. This pattern is expressed through phrases, such as *us versus them*, and labels, such as *legal* versus *illegal*. The reflections of Tracy L., an anti–illegal immigration activist whom I introduce in the next section, illustrate this split.

2. *Difficulties with Self and Identity*: According to Linehan, people who suffer from the condition of BPD grapple with a confused or incoherent sense of self. Borderline individuals often look to the environment for cues on how to act and even "what to think and feel."[14] Because these individuals gravitate toward either-or dichotomous thinking, they are unable to consider themselves as relational beings, capable of shifting identities and edges. One example of this difficulty can be seen with US citizens who experience moments of vulnerability through economic crisis or social displacement. These individuals may fail to recognize the experiences they have in common with undocumented immigrants or border crossers. The story of Shawna Forde, the former leader of Minuteman American Defense, a citizen action group, reveals this dilemma.

3. *Interpersonal Isolation and Alienation*: Linehan points out that "Isolation, alienation, feelings of being out of contact or not fitting in at all" are all examples of dialectical failures in which the sufferer of BPD has constructed a brittle self-other dichotomy.[15] What the BPD sufferer fails to grasp is the condition of *both-and*. An individual can maintain a sense of self and still be integrated into his or her environment—both are possible. The case of Jared Loughner highlights this self-other dichotomy.

Although I use each of the following case studies to highlight a particular instance of dialectical failure, it is important to note that within each example, the other elements also exist. However, I use these three examples to highlight different aspects of my application of Linehan's theory.

Dialectical Failure in the Borderlands: Three Examples

I. Tracy: A Case of Social Splitting

The most intense expressions of social splitting in southwest Arizona are found in the heated spaces of immigrants' rights protests (as described in Chapter 1). I also found that such either-or models of organizing the world were present in everyday conversations, within the distribution of social space, and, on a subtler level, in whether people chose to speak with me. I also found myself in many situations where I could not simply be an observer. Once, on my way to an immigrants' rights protest, I casually mentioned to an acquaintance that I had planned to observe the protest. He chastised me and shook his head in disbelief, "Observe? *Observe?*" with the full expectation that I was going to participate in the protest and march in solidarity with everyone else. When I found myself in situations that represented the two main camps of thinking, I tried not to attach myself to one side or another so that I could better understand all sides of the argument. I found that the dominant two sides had their own ways of explaining events, processing incidents, and describing the world at large. To my dismay I discovered that spending much time with members of one group gave reason for another group to distrust me. This situation made it difficult for me to connect with activists who were against illegal immigration (the progressives described them as "anti-immigration activists and racists"). One of these people with whom I tried to connect was Tracy.

I first met Tracy in front of the day laborer workplace on the south end of Phoenix. John and I went to the day laborer center so I could see the arrangement and see if there were any nativist activists in the area. Tracy was a woman in her early fifties, of average height, dark hair, and wearing sunglasses. Camped outside the day laborer center, she stood alone, supplied with guns, ammunition, and signs that read, "Illegals go home," and "Criminals and criminal activity." To her left, a dozen or more Latino men sat under a raised tarp, in shelter from the menacing sun, while waiting for work at the center. Going up to Tracy made me uneasy, especially with the dozen men looking on with disdain. I wound up having a brief conversation with her, and she explained her position as follows:

Nicole: So, why are you out here?

Tracy: It's not fair, and it's not right. I am unemployed. I have no job. I am a vet. I have no health insurance. And here all these guys are. Look at them—all piled up over there. [*She shook her head in disgust.*]

Nicole: Why do you think this happens?

Tracy: The government. Big business. The government just lets businesses do whatever they want. US citizens, we can't even make a living. Then these people come here, and it's bad for them, too. They come here and work for next to nothing. And it drives down our wages, too. They're being used.

Nicole: But if everyone is getting screwed, don't you have things in common then? Shouldn't you be working together?

Tracy (shaking her head and waving her hand in dissent): That's not the issue. That is not my concern. They need to stop coming over. If they stop coming over and stop breaking the law, these big businesses wouldn't have all these people they could use to their advantage. They are not just undocumented workers or border crossers. It is a crime, they know what they are doing; they are criminals and illegal aliens. . . . I am out here protecting my country. These illegals come here, through breaking the law, and get all kinds of free benefits. They go to school for free, they come here and expect all kinds of handouts. And I'm not supposed to protect my country? [The place] where I was born and raised? I've gone to war, and I came back. Now I have no job, nothing. They're not heroes—we are the real heroes. They [border crossers] are criminals, breaking into our country, and we just let 'em. They are criminals; they are breaking the law. That is wrong. That is why I am out here every day, doing the same thing—over and over.

Nicole: Don't you have something in common with undocumented immigrants?

Tracy: Now see, you just called them "undocumented immigrants." They're illegal aliens. They know what they're doing is wrong. And that don't matter if we have something in common with them. That's their problem. They're still illegal.

It was clear that, at least in a general way, Tracy understood the dynamics of a globalized economy. "Big business," as she described it, had the freedom to exploit the desperation of workers and use it to its advantage. This desperation drives wages down and affects the potential wealth and living standard of citizens in the United States. For Tracy and people who share her sentiment, border crossers represent job loss and the demise of the American standard of living. Although Tracy and border crossers share experiences of economic loss and exploitation, Tracy's worldview does not provide the room for solidarity. Instead, Tracy dismissed the similarity and emphasized the difference, thereby reinforcing the social split.[16] Tracy's perspective is similar to the example of Jodie in Chapter 1, who views the provisions that undocumented immigrants may receive as an "unfair exploitation of taxpayer funds." Like Jodie, Tracy also identifies the "illegal alien" as a threat to her life and livelihood.

2. Shawna Forde: A Case of the Difficulties of Self and Identity

> There is a war going on here. Oh, we are in a war. These people, they're evil down here. They are the ones who are criminals. The people coming over the border—they're the innocent ones. Those racists that sit out there on the border watching it—policing it—they're the real criminals.

Jimmy, an activist with a local humanitarian group, made these remarks one afternoon over lunch. I wondered to myself: *How does this person know who is racist, and by extension, a criminal?* I repeatedly found myself attempting to understand the logic used by activists who used the discourse of race as the key explanation for the behavior of nativists in support of border enforcement. One of the most notorious accounts of "vigilante racism" is that of Shawna Forde. She was convicted in 2011 as the ringleader in two first-degree murder charges for the shootings of Raul Flores and his daughter, Brisenia. At the time, Forde was the leader of the citizen action group Minutemen American Defense (MAD), described as a "rogue group engaged in citizen border patrols."[17] Forde and two other members of MAD led an unauthorized home invasion into the residence of Raul Flores, whom the local police suspected of trafficking drugs. She currently awaits execution at the Perryville Women's Detention Center in Goodyear, Arizona.[18]

When we look at Forde's life and its history of violence, her formation of the militia group, MAD, and her participation in border vigilantism do not seem bizarre. Forde's own life and body are artifacts of suffering. Her life and current sentence on death row map the abuse, inequality, violence, and brutality that were essential components of her socialization in the formative years of her life. According to Shawna, she came from a fractured, abusive, economically strained childhood.[19] She was transferred through an assortment of foster homes and ended up in juvenile detention. Later on, after eventually leaving juvenile detention, lacking a high school diploma, and with virtually no financial resources, Shawna resorted to prostitution to survive.[20] Over the years, domestic violence and repeated incidents of humiliation became the backdrop of her everyday life. Years of abandonment, childhood brutality, and violence from intimate partners eventually drew Shawna to a place where a performance of conflict complemented its social and political geography. For Shawna, violence became an integral part of constructing a sense of self and navigating the social world. This repeated exposure to violence is what criminologist Lonnie Athens calls a process of *violentization,* whereby the "brutalized evolve into the brutalizers."[21] In violentization, individuals undergo "coarse and cruel treatment at the hands of others that produces a lasting and dramatic impact upon the subsequent course of their lives."[22] As Athens defines it, this process of violentization includes three levels of exposure to violence: violent subjugation, personal horrification, and violent coaching.[23] Shawna's cumulative childhood and adolescent experiences of physical abuse, psychological abuse, and neglect may have helped to nurture the social and psychological conditions necessary for the process of violentization to develop.

After Shawna was charged for the double murder, journalists, commentators, and progressive activists began to categorize Shawna as *criminal, evil, vicious,* and a "*monster.*"[24] Although these descriptions may have an emotional appeal, the use of such labels obscures the larger social and political context in which individuals like Shawna develop and emerge. She illustrates the extent to which people will go seeking a sense of belonging. Her experiences resemble what anthropologist Victor Turner described as *liminality,* an impermanent state of being "betwixt and between," neither here nor there.[25] Shawna, however, was in an indefinite state of liminality, resembling what Linehan terms a "difficulty with the self," an ongoing state of conflict and ambiguity requiring resolution. Like Shawna, Arivaca, the border town where she eventually set up camp, was a divided landscape: strong signals of patriotism, nationalism, and partisanship shared unstable ground with the everyday uncertainty of life in a border town. For someone like Shawna, who was a "broken person" with "borderline tendencies,"[26] the social climate of southwestern Arizona provided the conditions of possibility to enact hypernationalism and vigilantism. The border can be seen as a symbolic extension of Shawna, where the rhetoric of the homeland, metaphors of "breaking and entering," and the imagery of threats, swarms, and invocations of the biopolitical body are extensions of the geography of the self.

Extreme patriotism and allegiance offer victimized individuals like Shawna a space of belonging, retreat, and protection. They also provide individuals in distress with an opportunity to publicly express their experiences of vulnerability and pain through performance. Shawna's attorney, Erik Larsen, explained, "Pain is what makes Shawna Forde who she is … we carry it with us today the same way we carried it as a child." Shawna's experiences of poverty, neglect, and abandonment left her with few connections, likely resulting in feelings of displacement, bitterness, and alienation. Few, if any, media pundits and commentators attempted to understand Shawna's action based on her life history. Instead, they used derogatory labels, such as *wastrel,* and the racial slur of *white trash* to describe Shawna, further stigmatizing her and emphasizing her liminality.[27] While in solitary confinement, Shawna reflected on "the rawness of my situation" and how her experiences of abandonment by her mother and instability shaped her world:

> I feel like a naked child standing in a black pit surrounded by pure evil unable to protect myself when you say her name [Shawna's mother] … she gave birth to me and left me with friends who gave me to other friends. . . . I desperately wanted her to love me.[28]

This marginality helped to push her further to enact her sense of belonging literally on the physical edges of geopolitical imaginings, and Shawna herself understood this. In the following quote, she rationalizes her performance of violence:

> You can beat me, rape me, stab me, shoot me, shoot my husband, kick my cat, HOLD MY PAST AGAINST ME, slander me, gossip blog, report, put me in public square, strip me naked, and cast stones while I bleed from head to toe. . . . I will stay the course and lead in this fight with every once [sic] of my strength and conviction I have I will not waist it on matter [sic] that do not pertain to this very mission. It is time for Americans to lock and load.

Shawna's history demonstrates, on an individual level, how an ecology of people and things develops. Archaeologist Ian Woodward explains this ecological process as a symbiotic relationship that occurs between people and things, observing how "inanimate things within the environment act on people, and are acted on by people, in order to carry out social functions, regulate social relations, and give symbolic meaning to human activity."[29] This is exemplified in how the demarcation of the US-Mexico border acts as a catalyst for the practices of captivity and containment. To an extent, the border operates as a skin, a membrane that symbolizes where national identity begins and ends. It is both a metaphorical and literal "site of cultural and political power" where individuals who choose to assert their national identity have a tangible, concrete object from which to start. As one participant I spoke with said, "This is both our doorstep *and* our backyard." Thus, the border is not only a place imbued with meaning, but also a concrete object that allows individuals who perceive or feel a sense of danger to externalize that feeling, assert their national identity, protect themselves, and feel a sense of belonging. In this sense, the border functions as a pivotal mechanism within a larger social ecology of individuals, geopolitical ideologies, and subjective understandings. Like other objects of material culture, the border acts as a "marker of aesthetic and self-identity," where "the object is given meaning through the narrativization of broader discourses on self, identity, and biography which links aesthetics to ethics of self and social identity."[30]

Although Forde is an extreme example of this identification, her story is in harmony with the argument of sociologist Matt Wray that Anglo-Americans in lower socioeconomic brackets exist in a state of stigmatized liminality. They are racialized and spatialized by those in more privileged positions. Over the course of the past three decades, individuals who belong to the working class, the downwardly mobile, and persons who are categorized as the Anglo-American underclass, are frequently labeled *white trash*. Their marginality and liminality signal an acute emotional, economic, and social fragility. Those who are more privileged contain this difference through the linguistic, social, and spatial boundaries of ethnicity and class encapsulated in the term *white trash*. Wray asks the question, "Is this a story about a residual, disposable class, or one about a despised ethnoracial group?" The same question can be applied to people like Shawna, who perform the marginalization of the self at a physical geopolitical boundary.

Wray drives this point home when he observes, "As those that opted out of or were left behind in the wake of capitalist modernization, poor whites appear more like a caste than a class, and as such are thought to have no social worth and only regressive political tendencies."[31]

Thus, the descriptor of *trash* is a sticky one; that is, the stigmatization it carries clings to those to whom the label is applied. The label *white trash* is a descriptor that racializes and spatializes. However, the descriptor of *trash* circulates elsewhere as well, and it is especially assigned to border crossers, who are perceived to be nationally, ethnically, and socioeconomically different. Although US citizens share a common social realm and may even share some of the social and economic insecurity of border crossers, these similarities are reconfigured and erased to emphasize difference. This is what Elaine Scarry describes as "making and unmaking of the world," a re-creation of the social world to match certain ideological perspectives and destroy others.[32] Consequently, the border of the United States reveals the symptoms of a collective *borderline* condition, one produced by liminality and ambiguity. Attempts by citizens to fortify the border wall are a public performance of containing those who are perceived to be radically other and a source of pollution.[33] Geographer Juanita Sundberg addresses the ways in which supporters of border enforcement re-*conceptualize* and re-*present* the experiences of border crossers and their relationship to the land, and to individuals in the United States, as profoundly other or deviant. She analyzes how the personal items left behind by border crossers are described by nativists and environmentalists as *trash*. Because the label of *trash* is also attached to migrants, they are associated with trash and perceived by individuals as human "trash,"[34]—different, radically other, and undeserving of protection or rights.[35] By using this label, individuals attempt to order the world by relegating persons who are classified as liminal and *other* to lower states of being. This dynamic marginalizes individuals and creates risk factors that researchers frequently link to violence,[36] which is exemplified in the next case discussed, Jared Loughner.

3. Jared Loughner: A Case of Interpersonal Isolation and Alienation

After the Tucson shooting, commentators throughout the United States scrambled to find an explanation for Jared Loughner's behavior. In nearly every discussion, the most frequently used words were *insane* and *crazed*. In an article on the news blog *Salon*, Laura Miller, a senior writer for the news site, describes what she believes to be the ridiculous reaction of people who look for clues in Loughner's writing and reading materials for his seemingly irrational behavior. She argues,

> Loughner is almost certainly insane, and like the countless other mentally disturbed people who send similar ravings to media outlets around the world, his ideas would have been ignored as incoherent and irrelevant if he hadn't fired a gun into a crowd of people on Saturday. The fact that he did fire that gun, however, doesn't make his delusions suddenly meaningful. . . . Crazy people who make headlines and change history are still crazy.[37]

Here, Miller assumes that Loughner's delusions were not meaningful. Instead, she stereotypes him as one of the many "mentally disturbed people" who exhibit irrational behavior. She fails to grasp that these symptoms are signals of suffering, something that Linehan recognizes. What seems to be incoherence or "craziness" to an outside observer may actually be the result of grappling with a dialectical failure. After the shooting, Loughner was diagnosed with paranoid schizophrenia, a condition characterized by disorganized speech and thought processes, hallucinations, and asociality. These symptoms give us some insight into his social world. If we examine Loughner's behavior through a dialectical model, we can attribute his internal struggle, incoherence, breaks with reality, and eventual violence to a destructive self-other opposition. As Linehan and others point out, if a person suffers from these conditions and the conflict is not resolved, the lack of resolution leads to self-destructive behaviors; in some cases (like this one), these behaviors become externalized onto the surrounding world, and they result in destructive behavior toward others.

Loughner's experiences prior to the shooting may help to explain the conditions of possibility that enabled him to commit violence. Alienation, or isolation, and inability to fit into his social group, seemed to be one of the key factors that set the stage for Loughner to explode in a violent act. One former close friend of his, Bryce Tierney, observed that Loughner felt more and more isolated and withdrawn from family and friends. Moreover, he spent more and more time focusing on his dream state, once declaring

"I'm a sleepwalker—who turns off the alarm clock."[38] Tierney explained that Loughner felt trapped and sought escape and alternative possibilities in the realm of dreams. He said Loughner realized "that when you're dreaming, you can do anything, you can create anything," and that "Loughner probably wanted to take everyone out of their monotonous lives ... to take people out of these norms that society had us trapped in."[39] One reporter further explained, "The evidence and reports about Mr. Loughner's unusual conduct suggest an increasing alienation from society, confusion, and anger, as well as foreboding that his life could soon come to an end."[40] Loughner's story elucidates how polarized environments provide few spaces of relief for individuals who experience disconnection or liminality. In Loughner's case, this failure stemmed from the detachment and deep isolation that he experienced in his own community and his belief that "the government was fucking us over."[41]

Loughner's extreme acts elicited a response from public and media commentators who questioned the increasing polarization found within the social and political environment at large. However, Loughner's former friend, Tierney, offers us a clue to what may have also been the catalyst for Loughner's response. That is, a rigid social environment may nurture the development of violence in certain communities; Tierney observed that Loughner might have wanted to "take people out of these norms that society had us trapped in." This experience of being *trapped* or *stuck*, as my participants described, has its roots in a dialectical failure in the social world.

Dialectical Failure as "Civil War"

In the late summer of 2012, my fiancé and I were at the home of some close acquaintances in Phoenix. As usual, the intense heat of the afternoon sun drove everyone inside. Six of us retreated to the dining room discussing local politics and, eventually, war and its relationship to problems in thinking patterns and "consciousness." To my surprise, the discussion turned into a prediction of civil war:

> *Nicole:* What do you think about using the idea of war regularly? It comes up in conversation every day—at least I think so—
>
> *Reynaldo:* Nah ... no one knows what to do about it. I think a war is coming—

Piper (interrupting Reynaldo): What the fuck? There's a war on every damn thing. We need to talk about something else besides war, but I don't know what that is. But for sure war divides us. War makes them against us. What the fuck?! It's frustrating to be down here. But I have nowhere else to go. I'm too broke anyway.

Diego: I think—I *know* a civil war is coming.

Reynaldo: It's already started.

Piper: Seriously, it has.

Nicole: Really? Why? I'm wondering if there is some other idea besides war to talk about what is going on down here.

Reynaldo: No. We can't. It's a war, the Chicanos are right. Look I'm not involved in all that activism down here. I used to be, but I don't want to be anymore. Sure, I'm Mexican American, and even I got tired of all the drama. Some people are sincere, and others, well ... you know—

Piper: They're just in it for the glory. Then there are the real activists who aren't in it for the glory. Like Eric. That guy is a workhorse. He's diabetic and everything, but he is the first and last person out there all the fucking time. He's even out there more than the Chicanos!

Reynaldo: Yeah, but anyway. We can't stop the war thing. I don't think we can. I don't know if I even want to. Because there is a racial war, a war on the poor ... class warfare. There's psychological warfare. Seriously, it's all about war here.

Carlos: It's Birmingham all over again. Ground Zero.

Piper: Yeah, Ground Zero.

Nicole: So, no other word you can think of?

Diego: Nope, because those fuckers are trying to kill us off!

Piper: But we need some other word. This shit cannot go on! I'm sick of it!

Diego: It's because this whole political system is a magician's show. The people are sleeping. Personally, I think all the activists on the left are funded by the right. How else can you do years of nothing?

Piper: How the fuck do people get their news from Stephen Colbert and Jon Stewart? They're just getting paid to be rodeo clowns. Didn't Rachel Maddow and Ann Coulter work together in the past? I think they were friends.

Renee: There needs to be a shift in consciousness.

Diego (walking away): Ha! Well that's not happening anytime soon.

Nicole (to Renee): Consciousness?

Renee: Yes, peoples' thinking needs to change.

Nicole: How?

Renee: Some major shift is going to have to happen. There's some kind of rupture now.

Diego (shouting from the living room): People need to die off. That's how!

Piper: Something is going to have to shift. We're stuck. We need to move on. Shit, maybe this 2012 thing will take care of it. Who knows?

In this exchange the theme of fixedness, or the *stuck* conditions of the social and political environment of southwestern Arizona, emerges. Being *stuck,* or in Linehan's terms, in *continuous conflict,* is the source of dialectical failure, and it potentiates the use of violence. Like the condition of a person who suffers from BPD, this irresolvable situation produces an ongoing internal conflict within the community—what Diego describes as a *civil war.* This point is driven home when Carlos uses the phrase *Ground Zero,* a phrase originally used to describe the bombing of Japan during World War II. He repeatedly used this term over the course of my fieldwork to describe the volatile state of politics and daily life in Arizona.

Conclusion: Understanding the Borderline as Diagnostically "Borderline"

In this chapter, I have used the psychological diagnosis of borderline personality disorder to understand the larger patterns of collective behavior in the southwestern region of Arizona. Although I do not assume that specific individuals have BPD, I do assert that the collective behavior of people in this region resembles the symptoms of this disorder. This mimicry is significant, because the explanation of BPD offered by Linehan provides us with the tools to understand conflict and identify potential risk factors for violence. Social phenomena, such as splitting, alienation, and difficulty with identity, are all important characteristics of what constitutes dialectical failure. By applying Linehan's framework, we can determine that the border is a social artifact that represents the condition of dialectical failure and, according to participants, amplifies violence. As Dan (whom I quote at the beginning of this chapter) observes, the border "creates more problems"; it concretizes an *us versus them* mentality and marks who is legal and who is illegal. Dichotomous thinking ignores the larger context of the social world as a living organism, and it weakens a person's ability to cope with paradoxical aspects of life, thereby creating a split in the social world. This split is how individuals emerge as agents who work for the state—in other words, de facto soldiers—a predicament that interviewees describe as *war*. How this condition reveals itself in the physical environment is the topic of my next chapter.

Chapter 5
Walls of Indifference
Encampments and Exclusion

December 2008

While speeding down Interstate 10, I fidget in the passenger seat and listen to Carlos provide a laundry list of grievances. With National Public Radio on in the background, he reports the "inhumane" and "sickening" behavior of local Phoenix residents who "lack any compassion for people who are struggling and suffering." Carlos throws his hands up in the air and releases his grip on the steering wheel. He explains that residents in Arizona are "apathetic." Folks "just don't care" and border crossers are regularly maltreated or left for dead. With increasing agitation, he notes the "callous nature" of Phoenix residents. He tells this story:

> Things here are really bad. I mean really bad! You know, a woman here was pregnant and went into labor. Because she didn't have any papers [undocumented] they wouldn't let her into the hospital. She had her baby out on the street. The other day, a friend told me that they found a man walking near the border with an IV in his arm. Apparently he was sick enough to be admitted, but once they found out that he was undocumented, they just dropped him off at the border. Abandoned him, just like that.

The next summer while exercising at a gym in Phoenix, I happened to mention to Stan, one of the personal trainers, the nature of my fieldwork. His face stiffened. He looked at me and said, "That's a very sad situation, but those illegals are a pain in the ass." Defiantly, Stan expressed his distaste for border crossers. He stated that the government needed to protect the border with physical force:

> All these illegals coming over . . . they want to bring everyone over—every family member. I can't afford that. I know how to speak Spanish. I made an effort to learn. I went to Spain and learned the language. I didn't get coddled. People like to say we're racist. You probably think so, too. But honestly, it can't go on like this. . . . Look at all the trash they leave in the desert. It's fucking disgusting! Shoot them all. They're just tearing the nation down. Everyone crossing the border illegally should be shot. The police needs to take them out. Each and every one of them should be shot.

These two conversations were especially memorable for me. I recall being struck by what I began to think of as an unrelenting divergence of opinions. Although the perspectives are so different, each speaker points to the split found within the social and physical environment. Carlos emphasized the detrimental effects of the social split between being documented and undocumented—a division that produces what he believes to be inhumane conditions for border crossers. In contrast, Stan acknowledges the split, sees its functionality, and supports the extermination of border crossers. This phenomenon of social splitting—in this case, the split between legal and illegal—is an example of the dialectical failure that persists in the borderlands. In my previous chapter, I argued that the border wall is a monument to this condition. In this chapter, I elaborate on that idea to map the social, psychological, and physical consequences of this borderline condition.

In the introduction, I pointed to the connection between Paul Gilroy's notion of the *camp mentality* and Giorgio Agamben's discussion of the *camp*. Agamben describes the camp as the *nomos,* or the organizing principle by which we construct modern reality. The camp is the "space that is opened when the state of exception [the threshold] has become the rule" and has a "permanent spatial arrangement."[1] Similarly, in *Against Race: Imagining Political Culture beyond the Color Line,* Gilroy analyzes what he describes as the *camp mentality,* the contemporary social practice of carving up the world into groups with fixed, unchangeable identities that leave little, if any, room for "in-betweenness," hybridity, and ambiguity.[2] In this chapter, I argue that, in order to exist, the ecology of militarization relies on the camp mentality in the form of a host of fixed and, presumably, unchanging identities. This is *the* practice that allows the emergence of social exclusion, physical encampments, and the constructions of walls. I argue that what we are seeing take place in Arizona is a prototypical manifestation of Agamben's literal camp that becomes possible through the social configuration of fixed identities. I illustrate this point with three examples: (1) the tension that exists among the Tohono O'odham, border crossers, and the US government; (2) public perceptions of migrants in connection with *trash*; and (3) the focus on encampments and the construction of material walls. Because of these factors, individuals easily rationalize structured indifference and assist in the production of death. I will elaborate first on the connection between Agamben's notion of the *camp* and Paul Gilroy's concept of the *camp mentality*.

"Ecologies of Belonging"—Identity and Camp-Thinking

In *Homo Sacer*, Agamben describes the Nazi concentration camp as the situation in the contemporary world "in which the most absolute *condition inhumana* that has ever existed on earth was realized."[3] He describes the camp as a place to capture and contain bodies—a space for mere warehousing and eventual death. The camp is thus a technology used to contain individuals perceived as "matter out of place."[4] Agamben further explains that instead of seeing the camp as an aberration or a relic of the past, we should consider the camp "as the hidden matrix" or basis of the environment in which we now live.[5]

Gilroy elaborates on this phenomenon by introducing the idea of the *camp mentality*. He situates the camp mentality as an integral part of modernity where new roles are defined for *citizen-soldiers* who connect to a "distinctive ecology of belonging."[6] This initially materialized in the form of national and governmental places of containment—that is, the nation-state. This affected how individuals perceived themselves and the worlds in which they lived. Here is where Gilroy differs from Agamben: he extends the notion of the camp to the nation-state itself. Gilroy argues that in order for the death factory to exist, physical areas of containment (camps) must exist first. These places of containment can only emerge through the formation of camp mentalities—the multiplicity of ways in which we construct our sense of self through concepts such as race, nation, ethnic difference, class, political affiliation, and numerous other categories. These categories, or *camp mentalities,* are what we currently recognize as *identities.*

In the following section, I explore some specific effects of using categories that designate social difference as identity. I show how conflating social differentiation with identity can contribute to the development of a camp mentality. As pointed out in my previous chapter, the existing social environment consists of camps and resembles an individual with borderline personality disorder. It is composed of conflicting, diametrically opposed structures that are in a continual state of quarrel with each other with no end in sight. In this social landscape, one is either legal or illegal, criminal or citizen, liberal or conservative, rich or poor, us or them. There is little, if any, allowance for hybridity—or as Gilroy describes it, *in-betweenness.* In other words, when the social landscape is sculpted into fixed or unchanging identities that are especially informed by the discourse of race, the social world is transformed into a "deadly, exclusionary force"—*encampments.* This is the space where the dehumanization of individuals can be fully realized in everyday life.

Thus, when identity camps solidify, they become parts that assist in the mechanization and depoliticization of citizen-subjects. This allows the movement "toward the totalitarian condition of permanent emergency" and becomes a way in which extremity is "instrumentalized."[7] This has profound social and psychological effects on individuals (especially those in the activist communities), where they are reduced to states that resemble mere existence, or *bare life.* Gilroy recognizes this problem and offers a possible corrective: he identifies the state of *in-betweenness* as the place that yields the most promise and stimulates synthesis and change. The "in-between locations ... represent opportunities for greater insight into the opposed worlds that enclosed them."[8] In other words, these in-between spaces are visionary, imaginative places that can be used to produce radical transformation.

Yet what happens when that state of in-betweenness is erased or classified as deviant? For individuals who decide to cross the US-Mexico border, this question becomes a matter of life and, all too frequently, death. By surreptitiously crossing the political boundary into the United States in lieu of documentation, border crossers move into what Agamben calls the "zone of indistinction between outside and inside, exception and rule, licit and illicit, in which the very concepts of subjective right and juridical protection no longer made any sense."[9] In the polarized social and political climate of Arizona, these "concepts of subjective right and juridical protection" break down and leave the migrants in the state of mere existence, or what Agamben refers to as *bare life*.[10] Border crossers transition into the state of bare life through two main avenues of exclusionary logic. In one, the newly encountered social and juridical realm, crossers participate in activities that are perceived as acts of transgression and contamination. In the second, because of the crossers' transgression and liminal condition, citizens often view them as deviant—an idea I discuss next.

The Logic of Exclusion I: Deviancy through Transgression

Supporters of border enforcement often use the idea of transgression to describe people who cross the border wall. Transgression emerges in a variety of forms, including a few that I have described in an earlier chapter—particularly with the theme of crime and *breaking and entering*. In the summer of 2009, I accompanied Dr. Jason De León to his Migrant Material Culture Project, based in Tucson. De León examined the relationship between the migrants and the objects they chose to supply themselves with for their passage through the Sonoran Desert. However, these zones in the harsh Sonoran Desert, referred to as *lay-up sites*, are actually places where border crossers stop to rest, change clothes, clean up, and take time to eat and/or sleep. Due to the stress and strain from traveling through the desert from Mexico and elsewhere, travelers eventually discard items that are of value to them. Objects I have found at lay-up sites include toothbrushes, underwear, deodorant, food wrappers, empty bottles of water, blankets, foot powder, children's shoes, toys, wallets, Bibles, and memorabilia. As I mentioned in the Introduction, border crossers often travel through lands that are in the jurisdiction of the Tohono O'odham, an indigenous group whose lands encompass a large area of southwestern and central Arizona. My observations there illustrate some of the contradictions that emerge from the use of this exclusionary logic based on trespassing and transgression.

Figures 18 and 19   Lay-up sites in the Sonoran Desert.

The following example took place while I was stationed in Tucson. One Sunday, I accompanied Sam and Edward, two members of the Tohono O'odham nation on their weekly trip into reservation territory. Sam and Edward are also volunteers for the group Good Neighbors, an organization committed to saving the lives of people who attempt to cross the border. I spent the day with them while they placed water in areas on the reservation known for having high traffic of border crossers. We started early, around 5:00 a.m., as Sam and Edward discussed plans for the day and began to provide me with the day's schedule and what would need to be done. Sam showed me a map of the Sonoran Desert, where we were going. The map illustrated the vast terrain of the desert, including the Baboquivari Mountains—the sacred land of the Tohono O'odham—and the border, the location where Sam was going to cross over into Nogales, Mexico. There he would refill the large water barrels at the station set up by Good Neighbors to ensure that border crossers would have fresh refills of water on their treacherous trek through the desert. While we drove out onto the long serpentine roads, he reminded me,

Now don't help us put water out on the desert. I'm asking you not to. I don't want you to get arrested. We can put water out here because we're Tohono O'odham and the rules will not apply to us. But if the Tohono O'odham police see you here putting water out here on the land, you'll get arrested. The tribal council disapproves of this work, and they will arrest non-Tohono folks. So don't get yourself into trouble.

The Tohono O'odham are an indigenous people who live in central and southern Arizona. Their reservation lands consist of 4,453 square miles, reaching up to the Phoenix metropolitan areas and extending to the boundary between the United States and Mexico. There are also several thousand Tohono O'odham in communities on the other side of the US-Mexico border in Sonora, Mexico. The international boundary interferes with the lives of people who have migrated through the desert for centuries. According to the tribe's website the border acts as "an artificial barrier to the freedom of the Tohono O'odham" whereby they are unable to "traverse their lands ... collect foods and materials needed to sustain their culture, and ... visit family members and traditional sacred sites."[11] These contemporary geopolitical boundaries have impinged on the lives of tribal members to such an extent that, as one participant noted, the Border Patrol has even targeted and deported some Tohono O'odham while they were migrating through their native homelands.

Sam explained that migrants who cross the desert through the Tohono O'odham lands are not welcome. He described the tribe's predicament and the reasoning behind their position:

> They don't approve of this work. Sometimes I'll put water jugs out here, and I'll come back and see them slashed open. They don't want border crossers here. Some folks even say, "Let them die out there in the desert. They shouldn't be crossing here in the first place." You see, when people cross the desert and they wind up being picked up by the Tohono O'odham police, if they're really sick, they wind up being taken to the tribal hospital. Now, the tribal hospital works on a limited amount of funds annually. If border crossers wind up being sick out here, with say, hyperthermia, well, they're not Tohono O'odham. The tribal hospital winds up paying for that out of pocket. They don't get reimbursed for taking care of the people they find out there. That's money lost and could have been used for one of the Tohono O'odham people. So now

Figure 20   The demilitarized zone between the United States and Mexico on the Tohono O'odham reservation.

they are just saying, "Let them die out there. We can't afford to take care of them." I can't argue with that; they are right. This will eat up tribal funds. But this is also immoral—to let people just die out there. And as long as people are going to be crossing the desert, I will keep putting

Figure 21   Water placed in the desert for border crossers by humanitarian activists.

water out here. But I can't argue with them. They are trying to help our people. But they do have a point—they *do* have a point. Some jugs will probably get slashed, but others will be opened by some poor soul trying to cross the desert. Every time I find the ring from the cap of one of those jugs, I think to myself, *This water may be saving someone's life.* That's what keeps me going.

Sam describes the dilemma of the Tohono O'odham when individuals who attempt to cross the border through reservation land encounter life-threatening situations. Although public discussions of border crossers tend to focus on a dualistic, black-and-white framework, there are far more ambiguous relationships at work that participants reflect on in private. For the Tohono O'odham, the consequences of colonization and its by-product—the eventual configuration of the nation-state and the demarcation of reservations—result in contradictory goals. The encampments of the nation and of reservation land result in practices of exclusion; space and place are carved up segments where a policy of letting some individuals die for the sake of others becomes a deadly rationality that haunts the landscape. What compels people to make choices that result in abandoning vulnerable individuals at risk of dying? This dilemma is a result of a camp mentality (in this case *tribal*), where indifference is rationalized and cultivated as a social and political practice. As Sam points out, the tribe's objective is to preserve funds for actual tribal members. However, this economic and political logic results in an indifference to death, a logic that is supported in other contexts by tropes of contamination, my next subject.

Logic of Exclusion II: Deviancy through Contamination

A major point of contention in the borderlands regions of Arizona is the issue of *migrant trash*. When examined from a distance and removed from social context, these abandoned objects can indeed resemble a landfill or a dumpsite. People who cross the desert bring these items to sustain them over an extended period of time. However, as mentioned earlier, while under the stress and strain of a fifty-mile trek in the desert, migrants "are often in direct conflict with the social and somatic impacts associated with the use of those objects."[12] In other words, travelers frequently brought the necessary items for survival and mementos that would connect them to their home and families. In order to lighten their load, they frequently discard their objects in the desert. This is not the result of deliberate littering, but a consequence of desperation and physical exhaustion.

Environmentalists and many borderlands residents are disgusted by the scale of the items left in the desert and consider it *trash*. The negative perception of these objects has been an ongoing source of disagreement between various activist groups and local residents. Humanitarian groups, such as Ya Basta, argue that calling the items *trash* results in the stigmatization of migrants. As a result, the public then views migrants themselves as trash, as in the phrase *migrant trash*. Geographer Juanita Sundberg addresses the social disconnection exhibited by individuals in the United States who support border enforcement and the public at large. She analyzes the personal items left behind by border crossers that are described by nativists and environmentalists as *trash*, misconceiving and misrepresenting the reality of the relationship that border crossers have to the land. Migrants are then associated and perceived by the public as human *trash*,[13]—undeserving, disposable individuals. One participant, Casey, drove this point home:

> We've got to do something about this—all these people coming over. I mean do you see all that trash they leave out in the desert? Oh my God! It's disgusting! How can people live like that . . . they are filthy . . . how can you do this in someone else's home? What kind of person would choose to make their kids go through that? Living like animals?

Casey illustrates how migrants are easily associated with the objects they leave behind in the desert and are seen as unhygienic and a danger to the nation. By using the phrase "what kind of person would choose," Casey implicitly questions whether the people traveling through the desert are even human. From this viewpoint, border crossers *choose* to give up their political identity and *decide* to live like the "animals," thereby contaminating themselves. Thus, they are no longer worthy of protection or acknowledgment as human beings.

Casey's description highlights another important point: beyond the metaphors of trash and waste are the social and political meanings of the objects themselves. The objects found at these lay-up sites are social artifacts that record the condition of in-betweenness or liminality that I discussed earlier. When border crossers suffering from the stress and exhaustion of traveling through the desert decide to leave objects behind, they begin to record their descent into Agamben's *zone of indistinction*. Here is where they are no longer recognized as subjects of any state deserving of protection. As they shed the few items they carry, they strip themselves down to bare life. Thus when Casey used the phrase "living like the animals," she reveals her understanding of political subjectivity as explained in Agamben's use of the term *bare life*. When individuals classify the objects that border crossers leave behind as *trash*, they bring into question the humanity and worth of the border crossers themselves.

The label *trash* is a descriptor that is contaminating, and it assists in the rationalization of migrants as waste products of society that need to be managed.[14] This discursive practice is also a "technology of exile"; it is a social instrument of spatialization. In the collective imagination, border crossers are constructed as objects of pollution and a threat deserving of social and political exclusion. The consequences of this logic are indifference to suffering and social abandonment.

Consequences: Indifference and Abandonment

During Christmas vacation in 2010, I visited Gail and Michael, friends who live in a walled community a few miles outside of El Paso. I was intrigued by the location of their home; by walking outside of their apartment, I could easily see the massive border wall. Knowing of my interests in borders and walls, we drove down to the "the wall" that separated El Paso from Ciudad Juarez, Mexico. As we got out of the car, I was struck by the height of the wall; it towered over me. At least to my naked eye, it appeared to be an effective deterrent. "Wow, that fence is really high," I said, after taking some pictures. "Great," said Gail. "Now all we need is that fence to have an electrical shock." Surprised, I looked at Gail curiously. She quickly said, "Well, not shock them to death, but you know, just enough so they won't try to come over."

Gail's sentiment points to a phenomenon that Setha Low describes in *Behind the Gates: Life, Security, and the Pursuit of Happiness in Fortress America*. She evaluates the psychological effect of walls on residents who live in enclosed communities. Low observes that walls are indicative of a form of dualistic thinking, a form of "social splitting used to cope with anxiety and fear."[15] She further observes that dualistic modes of thinking may provide a tool that enables individuals to distance themselves "from

Figure 22   The US-Mexico Border. El Paso, Texas.

an undesirable self-image and project it on to another."[16] Gail's sentiments support Low's observation. For Gail, the walls allow psychological distancing; they are a formal representation of those who belong and those who do not. For those who do not belong, according to Gail, a massive border wall that has the ability to emit an electrical shock is an appropriate means of deterring border crossers.

Besides the typical defense mechanisms, such as projection, I also noticed that walls enable individuals to contract their awareness of the broader social and environmental problems that others face. Sister Roslin, a petite woman in her late sixties, explains how individuals are able to do so. Sister Roslin is a nun in a Jesuit order who worked in the 1980s in Nicaragua during the Sandinista War. Currently a volunteer at a borderlands detention center, Sister Roslin has heard countless stories of the trauma and suffering that detainees experience. She set her small frame on a chair and spoke for at least thirty minutes without pause, expressing her own grief and frustrations:

Figures 23 and 24   Walls near gated communities, adjacent to the border.

This is not easy work at all. You hear so many tragic stories. Like this woman from El Salvador. Her husband left her with two kids. She had no money. A hurricane hit her house. So she left her kids with her mother and moved to go to Mexico to get work. When she went there, she got gang raped in Mexico. She had nothing, nothing. She decided to try and cross the desert with a group. The Border Patrol saw her group and they got scared and scattered. She was walking alone, praying and crying. Asking God to help her live. She got caught, and while she was at the police station an officer screamed into her face, "Go back to your country, we don't want you here!" People are traumatized, mentally, emotionally, and spiritually. I've met beautiful people from all over the world. I have a lot of respect for the detainees. Although our mission is to locate and deport, even within that scope we can help them. But I think that is all kind of incidental ... we need to tell them that we are with them, to hear their stories. . . . What happens is that when they are here, they have so much time to think—they get desperate. . . . Mostly the detainees talk about wanting to see their families. I've seen so many women sobbing, crying, "I want to see my baby!"

Personally, I think that people who have passes to go through a PoE [port of entry] just come here and stay. And I can understand why. There was this other woman. She was pregnant. Armed people pushed themselves into her house. They killed her mother, her aunt, her brothers, and cousins. Everyone in the house—seven total. But she survived. She was hiding under the bed—pregnant! She's one of the lucky ones though. She actually had a visa. . . . People here—we talk about it all the time. It gets very depressing. You don't want to even open the newspaper. People are fearful, that it's [violence] going to come here. . . . It's like a schizophrenic existence. Sometimes I feel like I'm back in Nicaragua because it's like being in the Sandinista War. . . . People have difficulty understanding what it means to be on the border. I've heard people say, "They're always having problems *down there*." They're simply not involved in the situation. They have no emotional ties. There is a wall of indifference . . . but I think it's ignorance. I tell people when they criticize the immigrants, *Try to think of the root of the problem.*

Roslin observes the various levels of indifference that result in individuals rationalizing the abandonment of others. When citizens socially differentiate through the configuration of space, they create assorted forms of encampments, such as border walls and detention centers. This creation of physical encampments helps to sustain social practices of exclusion. It augments social splitting, the dualistic thinking that informs an *us versus them* mentality. Her description of a "schizophrenic existence" refers to the sense of disjuncture she experiences living in the border city. To her, the wall symbolizes a fractured and muted awareness: the wall functions as a visual tool of quasi containment where suffering is spatialized. It is a failed attempt to conceal the violence and suffering that bind the border cities together. For Sister Roslin, this exacerbates the violence and suffering for everyone. She later explains, "No one is safe . . . people are always fleeing across the border, escaping violence. It affects both sides of the border." Roslin underscored this point when she described the border wall as a "wall of indifference," a social barrier where the personal experiences of border crossers are inconsequential and constantly met with bureaucratic apathy.

For many immigrants' rights activists, the apathy has made human rights concerns even more urgent. The apathy underscores the vulnerable position of border crossers; they are stateless, unprotected, and lack the sympathy of local residents. In the next two examples, participants describe the condition that border crossers find themselves in as stateless individuals. Both speakers note the danger that border crossers face when they lack documentation and legitimate recognition by the state. The first story, told by Carlos, illustrates how undocumented individuals are endangered—especially women:

> We had an incident here. A lady was raped, and her child was abused as well during the same incident! But she didn't report it ... she was afraid. By reporting it, what could happen with her and her child? You know, she was afraid that she would be thrown in jail because she didn't have papers [undocumented]. See how this is? When people are afraid, you have an unsafe community.

Similarly, Brian, another interviewee whom I originally met in Seattle, described two incidents in a close friend's neighborhood:

> Sure there is crime in Phoenix. Everybody does bad things; it doesn't matter about race. Before I left Phoenix and came to Seattle, there were two guys I knew that really are criminals. They're both illegal, really terrible. One of the guys has a shitload of money running an illegal construction business. Do you know how he makes all that money? By ripping his employees off. He hires all these workers who have no papers either. So he puts them to work and refuses to pay them at the end of the gig and threatens them by saying they are illegal and will have someone turn them in to the Feds. So they have no one to complain to, or to report this bastard to. The other guy I know, I've heard from so many people that he molests his niece repeatedly, over and over. Disgusting. But now I'm moving back to Phoenix from Seattle. You bet if they're still there, I'm going to turn 'em in! Maricopa County is going to get a call from me. People like that should not be here.

Likewise, many people who work in social and human services understand the deleterious consequences of militarization and bureaucratic apathy that are now fixed aspects of living in the borderlands. The following exchange occurred during a conversation I had at dinner with two social workers I introduced in Chapter 3. Here, they reflect on their work with vulnerable populations and its emotional and somatic effects:

Social Worker 1: We see a lot of violence from Mexico, sexual abuse to females. PTSD [post-traumatic stress disorder]. Both men and women have it … coyotes are raping women. We get a lot of referrals for sexual violence, physical violence—it's terrible. It's hard because they [people fleeing] want asylum. I mean, they're running away from rapists and stuff … that's hard to refuse.

Social Worker 2: Oh they have nightmares—a lot! Flashbacks, night terrors, people shake, depression. Some are suicidal. But most have [suicidal] ideations. So much sleeplessness. What's worse is that, here, the detainees don't trust the guards. They associate uniforms with corruption. You know, the police in Mexico—they're corrupt. The violence is getting worse because the small businesses that used to be in Mexico are coming here. People close up their houses, close up their restaurants. Cartels are losing places to launder their money. So now they're terrorizing the people and trying to force them into giving them money.

Nicole: You mean extortion?

Social Worker 2: Yes, exactly—extortion. They come back every month—the middle of the night, during the day—whenever. I saw this one woman today. Her husband sent her over here for asylum protection and for medical help. It was so terrible. One of the cartel people left her for dead. They shot her in the head. But the bullet didn't stay in her head, it flew out. In a way that was good. But they left her for dead in front of her five-year-old. She was blinded by the head shot. Her baby was screaming, and she was blinded, couldn't see anything after she was shot. She was crawling across the floor, crawling across the floor, looking for her baby, bleeding. They left her for dead. She still doesn't have sight. She's getting better—her hair grew back, too. But you could still see the bullet marks in her head. But you know she's so upset, distraught. She's separated from her husband and her baby. [*Shakes her head and puts her head in her hands.*]

Social Worker 1: The system does not work. Why do people have to stay here for so long? All this detainment causes depression. People deteriorate … they have all that time to think and think and think. Even though it's not a prison, it's still the same concept. Same routine. It's hard for us to do our jobs. Court delays us. The clinic traffic (busy-ness) delays us. We don't have a lot of space here—there's no privacy, you know.

Social Worker 2: But I don't let this affect me.

Nicole: How do you deal with this?

Social Worker 1: Me? I go dancing.

Social Worker 2: I go running.

Social Worker 1: I've seen you cry.

Social Worker 2: But you can't cry! I go like this, like this! [*She pulls her lower eyelids down to let the tears dry out.*]

Situations like these abound—persons who need the help of state or social services are denied, ignored, or afraid to report abuses, because they are also identified as *criminals* who are undeserving and a threat to the state. The denial of emergency health care to unauthorized migrants, ongoing racial profiling, and use of GPS ankle bracelets to track and detain individuals are all aspects of a landscape configured and constructed by a rhetoric of fear. This logic helps individuals to sustain the conditions necessary for social exclusion and abandonment. As indicated in the two previous examples, with or without papers, many individuals live under chronic conditions of stress, vulnerability, and fear. These stressors further exacerbate what many residents describe as an "unsafe community" and become risk factors for further violence.

Consequences: The Price of Activism

Many of my participants recognized the need for change and understood that local activism is a useful instrument to publicize and dramatize the plight of disenfranchised communities. However, they also noted the detrimental effects of being immersed in activism. One participant said that he didn't have the "stomach" for protesting, that it was filled with people that had "bad energy" and who were "toxic." Other participants noted that it was "depressing," "scary," "too violent," or just "exhausting" and that they "couldn't take it anymore." Several interviewees described the paralysis they felt when they understood the gravity of the situation in Arizona. One of those individuals was Nadine.

I met Nadine in a store in one of the many new-age tourist traps in an alternative neighborhood in downtown Tucson. While I was inspecting a beautiful geode, a young woman greeted me cheerfully. We made small talk about Tucson, and she asked me where I was from. As it turned out, she was from the Pacific Northwest. When I mentioned to her that I had just come back from a patrol in the desert with a group that went out to look for migrants, her eyes widened. She whispered, "Is it a good group?" Confused, I looked at her blankly. She quietly asked, "I mean do you help them?" I said, "Oh yeah, we placed some water out in the desert and had some food and first aid packs, just in case." She sighed, placed her hand over heart and said, "Oh good, good."

It turned out that Nadine left the Portland area and moved down to Tucson after receiving her bachelor's degree in Spanish. She was happy to hear about my research. When I asked her if she would be interested in an interview, her eyes lit up. She quickly dropped her eyes, and her shoulders drooped forward as she shook her head. "It's scary, you know. I worked in a hospital and—*ugh*—what the migrants have to deal with is terrible. They [migrants] would ask me if I was taking down their address—there was this one woman who asked me. When I said, 'Yes,' she took the paper out of my hand and ripped it up. She never came back. But she needed help! They didn't have Social Security numbers or anything. But still, *still*!"

When I met Nadine the next day for an interview, she was anxious that I not use her real name or identify the clinic where she previously worked. For about a year, she had conducted intake for a public community clinic. The clinic offered free colonoscopies for individuals who were sixty years old and over. Approximately 75 to 80 percent of clinic patients were, as she described, "Hispanic." Nadine commented on the fear, frustration, and paralysis she experienced:

> *Nadine:* People would bring their Mexican ID with their name and stuff, you know? We didn't care. But you know, their addresses and information? That's going to the state government. I can't lie to them. You don't want them to get into trouble, but you don't want them going without health care. They need help, papers or not!
>
> You know, when I lived up North, all I knew about was Cinco de Mayo. But here, it's like, *Oh,* **now** I get it. It's easy to detach yourself from the immigration situation. Even here, in Tucson. It's segregated here. . . . I don't know if you would call it segregated. Maybe? But it's easy to get away from it [concerns of immigration]. I feel really protective of the migrants. These are people I care about. But I have a feeling of helpless-

ness. When she ripped up the papers and left without help, I cried. The feeling of dominance, the inequality. I felt helpless. It was my job to ask them for their name and Social Security number. . . .

I guess that experience was good for me. It's been good to take time out and pay attention to these things [referring to migrants and activist causes]. But the things that go on down here? It's an identity thing. It's the cool thing to do down here. In college, college is the place to get started in activism ... but you don't have to go out and join this or that group. It can be in your daily life. We can all be activists. We don't have to be protesting like crazy. We need an underground railroad kind of thing. But who can you totally trust if you were going to get involved in something like that? Because it's the exact same thing. Really, it's racism. Like in Germany, you know? This is really scary.

Nicole: Racism?

Nadine: Yes, but you know, when you use that word, there's no more dialoging. I had this friend; he called me a racist because I wasn't an activist! I felt very defensive. It means you're not caring, that it's your job to not be apathetic. I've been learning how to care, really being empathetic. But it hurts. The problems down here, I feel helpless. It's way too big for me to do anything really. I'm scared; I feel paralyzed. We need to manifest a different kind of situation.

Nadine echoes a feeling that several participants mention: the feeling of paralysis in the face of an overwhelming situation. She expressed her care for the migrants and "felt protective" of them. Yet at the same time, she expressed fear, emotional trauma, and helplessness. The expectation of some activists that an individual is obligated to take up a cause and assume it as an identity is troubling to her. Nadine also notes that not being an activist for immigrants' rights is equated with being a racist, an accusation she finds "hurtful." Nadine wants to participate, but also feels helpless, trapped, and frightened.

Father Timothy shares Nadine's ambivalence. Timothy is a Catholic priest who serves at a local chapel and supports a small parish community in a suburb of Phoenix. A native Arizonan of Mexican American ancestry, he often finds himself on the margins of activist communities:

Nicole, I'm not built for that kind of activism, so I don't go to the protests. The cursing, the violence, the hatred—all that anger! I know that people think I'm a cop out for not participating in their walks for peace and immigrant rights. But I know that some people have to step back and be supportive in other ways. That violence and hatred—it kills the soul. Imagine all these groups all worked up all the time; that can't be good for them! There are too many wounded people out there who are fighting out there in streets. There is too much hatred; it is not psychically good for me. I support people in my community in other ways.

Piper, a former activist whom I introduced in Chapter 2, recognized that some people "don't have the constitution" for the stress incurred by being immersed in activism. She explains, "I don't think some people can handle it. They're too fragile. Like Elsie. I can't imagine her being out there all the time. If she comes to a protest once a year that's good. I understand. I think that stuff would kill her; you could knock her over just by blowing in her direction. Some people are really fragile. It will make them sick!"

Jimmy, an activist who is affiliated with several humanitarian organizations, whom I introduced in Chapter 2, echoed this sentiment. He also commented on the everyday habits that he felt many activists share:

> You know what? Most activists are really unhealthy. A lot of them eat crap and smoke too much. I mean look at me, I smoke like a chimney. You know I used to be a fucked up guy. My life was really fucked up. I used to be an alcoholic; I did a lot of drugs. I've replaced a lot of my anger and energy when I was drinking my life away. I've replaced the high I get with alcohol with the high I get from activism and getting out there in people's faces. I've replaced one high with another. But I'm working for an important cause now. . . . Sometimes I'm out here every day, all day. But I'm out here for a reason ... somebody has to be. . . . I love getting in those racists' faces. They're disgusting! Getting *in* their faces. Shouting, screaming at them! I get a rush. Oh, I know, I've replaced one addiction with another!

Here Jimmy illustrates an observation that Piper and Timothy alluded to also: that keeping oneself continuously immersed in activism is unhealthy for the individual. People carry the "bad energy," "sick," and debilitating effects of activism in their bodies. Several activists recognized the dangers of being involved in activism, noting that they needed to "get away" because they were "losing perspective."

Consequences: Withdrawing from Activism

During my last visit to Arizona in January 2011, Carlos, the patriarch of my adopted family in Phoenix, left mainstream activism. Instead, he decided to become an ordained minister in order to combine his activism and spiritual interests:

> Honestly, since you've been gone, I've kept away from the activist world. I've stopped engaging with it for some time. It was affecting my health, making my diabetes worse. It's come to a standstill. There's too many egos involved. There are a lot of people behind SB 1070. It's really a stupid position, that bill. It's bankrupting the state. It's a dumbass thing to do … really destructive and discouraging. I think the corporate agenda is to create a slave working class. We took our money out of Wells Fargo. That bank profits off of the suffering of others. I am just working on getting ordained to have some credentials to increase outreach in our community. Nicole, it's really depressing. Nearly everyone I know, they're depressed. I've been depressed for years, but I try to keep my depression from getting out of control by doing outreach. Arizona is going to pay karmically for what it's done. At some point there will be a reckoning. We've just gotta play it out and see where it goes. Moving out of the [foreclosed] house is a big step down for us. We are downsizing and hope to get a new start. This just wasn't working out for us with the economy. It's a really sad deal.

On that same visit, Eric, an activist I introduced in Chapter 3, reported that a close friend of the activist community had committed suicide and that many activists were "in shock." Eric offered his own diagnosis of Arizona and expressed the damaging effects of the social, economic, and political climate of Arizona:

> You know Joe? He committed suicide. Left a note and everything. I feel like I'm in a chapter of Dante's *Inferno*. We are burning up down here. We've got to deal with something constructively. Find a way out of the abyss. We all knew Joe, and everyone is shocked. It was devastating … to have the realization that someone couldn't take it anymore. He was depressed about his financial situation. Broke. Depressed about the economy. Depressed about Jan Brewer getting elected—again. A few weeks ago we were commiserating about this, but I didn't know he

couldn't go on anymore. That's a whole new element. Nobody saw that coming. We never had a suicide before in the activist community. He had his issues, but he had a girlfriend, friends. This week, I heard the state is cutting back another 20 million in health care. We're doing ourselves in constantly because of our racism, our prejudices. It's sad. Arizona is a clinically depressed state.

Although each of the previous examples originates from a very different viewpoint, they all share the sentiment that the social climate of Arizona has deleterious effects on the individual: the social polarization facilitated by the political climate of Arizona affects a person's state of mind and has consequences in daily life. This suggests what sociologist Jackie Orr calls the "militarization of inner space." Whereas some individuals, such as Jimmy, seem more equipped to adjust to the social conditioning inherent in immigration activism, other people, such as Nadine, Timothy, and Carlos, are acutely aware of how this environment affects psychological and physical well-being. They acknowledge that the hostility, the politically charged nature of activism, and the habitual fighting and "violence and hatred" have tangible effects on local residents who choose to participate in activism. Consequently, many people choose to withdraw, even in the most extreme case—through suicide.

Consequences: Aestheticization of Suffering

For some, activism serves as a means that individuals, especially human rights activists, use as a form of social capital. This was a phenomenon I witnessed regularly while out in the field. Protesting and volunteering— especially if someone "rescued" a person or "found a body"—became quantifiable ways by which activists accrued social power and which were translated into acts of heroism. Over coffee, Krista, an activist based in Phoenix, observed,

> Activism does weird things to people. We're not heroes or anything. Some people like to think they are. This is a moral obligation; I mean we have to do this! People are dying all the time out there. But, you know, I try to stay away from all the egos. You can lose perspective really easily. There

are a lot of people that are really ego driven. They like the fame. I try to be humble and just stay in the background and make posters, be low key, stuff like that. I don't go out into the desert to find bodies or anything, because life is sacred. Finding someone's body is a serious thing. Their soul is out there and needs to be put to rest. Some people think it's a big deal ... well it is, but you need to be humble about it.

There are also activists who live in other states and travel to the borderlands to volunteer. Although well intended, their intermittent presence has unintentional effects. Nadine and several individuals recognized this problem within the activist communities. One participant in particular, Edward, noticed the financial advantage and emotional detachment that nonresidents exhibit. I met him during my visit to the Tohono O'odham reservation, a visit I mentioned earlier in this chapter. The "volunteers" who generally behaved like tourists angered Edward. He found the influx of researchers, students, and journalists who came "looking for a thrill" especially infuriating. Edward was wary of my research and was understandably annoyed by the endless stream of student volunteers who vacationed in the desert. During one conversation we had the following exchange:

> *Edward:* What are you going to do with your research? Are you like the rest of those people, who come down here, get their story, and just leave? What are you going to give back?
>
> *Nicole:* I don't know. I should ask my advisor what she did with the proceeds of her book. What do you want me to do? What do you want me to give back?
>
> *Edward:* Tell people to stop coming down here looking to have fun. Because this work is not fun. It's not a vacation. This may be their vacation, where those kids come down here looking to do some volunteer work and wanting to have fun, but we're talking about people's lives here. These people, they come down here looking for thrills. They say they come down here wanting to help. Then they get mad when they don't see a "runner," or a dead body. I heard people get mad and complain, "I didn't see a runner," or "where are the dead bodies?" Like they're looking for death. It's disrespectful to the dead. To us. To the land. Tell these people who want to visit that—not to come down here and be disrespectful.
>
> *Nicole:* I can do that. [*Edward nods and walks away.*]

While I stood there taking Edward's counsel, Sam tapped me on the shoulder. "Yeah, Edward's a tough one," Sam said. "He's been through a lot. He's right though; a lot of people come down here looking for a thrill. You know, like it's a movie or something. But it's hot down here, and people suffer. In the summer, this is no place for anyone. Out here, the sun just fries your head, and it's hot. Hotter than hell." Prior to Edward's comments, I had already begun to wonder why some people were interested in traveling to the desert over spring break or summer vacation. But not until Edward said this was I able to recognize what I had been feeling for months before—that people view the borderlands as being on the edges of civilization. The borderlands are danger zones, places of chaos and adventure.[17] Consequently, for some volunteers, their humanitarian activities also served as a de facto form of tourism. Once, after a guest-speaking engagement where I discussed the US-Mexico border, a student approached me and said excitedly, "I was down there [Tucson] over spring break. It was okay; I was kind of disappointed, though—we didn't see any dead bodies." Her comment reminded me of Edward's counsel and objections. Under the guise of humanitarian work, students, researchers, and journalists unwittingly participate in a tourist economy that emerges from the social production of death. This academic tourism also is a hand-maiden for routinized indifference that trivializes the suffering of border crossers. As Sister Roslin points out, individuals who do not live in or near the borderlands are able to emotionally detach themselves from the lived experience, and they often depict aestheticized and romanticized experiences that resemble an urban safari. Visiting the borderlands over one's spring break and looking for "dead bodies" is not the same as experiencing the sustained misery that local residents face daily and do not necessarily have the privilege of escaping.

Conclusion: Liminality, Deviance, and the Spellwork of the State

In this chapter, I have examined how the condition of dialectical failure manifests in borderland communities. This occurs through the construction of fixed, unchangeable identities. This state is what Paul Gilroy refers to as the *camp mentality*. When framed in dialectical terms such as *us versus them, rich versus poor, legal versus illegal,* these identity camps are developed within the psyche of individuals. This psychological conditioning enables individuals to carve up space and place in ways that force individuals to group into polarized camps of belonging. Although the values of immigration rights activists attempt to disturb the extreme perspectives of nativists and of individuals who support fortification of the US-Mexico border, much of the rhetoric of immigration activists reinforces the extant social and political divisions. As participants explain, they find the polarized environment to be highly charged and *toxic,* to the extent that some find it psychologically debilitating. As a result, they have chosen to consciously disengage from mainstream activism. Similar to border crossers, these individuals exist in a state of *in-betweenness,* and they struggle with the plight of socially existing outside of activist camps. This in-betweenness, or liminality, is outside of bounds of acceptable formations of identity and viewed as deviant and morally questionable. The condition of liminality is most exemplified in the plight of border crossers. They have few, if any, laws that protect them, and they are viewed by many to be undeserving of the most basic of needs. This social and political practice of exception emerges by categorizing any form of liminality—or, in Gilroy's words, the condition of *in-betweenness*—as deviant. Anthropologist Victor Turner described the condition of liminality as a state of being neither here nor there or, "betwixt and between." This state, sometimes encountered as a rite of passage, occurs at the *limen*—the *threshold*. Persons at the threshold did not stay there indefinitely. According to Turner, one passed eventually into a new social state of being and was then integrated back into society.[18] What Turner did not address was the plight of individuals who remained in indefinite states of liminality, such as border crossers who suffer in a "no-man's land" of ambiguity.[19]

Social theorist Michel Foucault speaks about this situation in his article, "Of Other Spaces." In this article, he describes a social place that he calls a *heterotopia,* a place of otherness. He describes heterotopias as functioning in two main ways. Heterotopias can serve as "privileged or sacred or forbidden places ... which are reserved for individuals in a state of crisis."[20] In other words, a heterotopia is a sanctuary space designated for individuals experiencing emergency or transition in relation to society. For Foucault, persons undergoing transition are liminal individuals, including adolescents, pregnant women, the elderly, and a variety of others experiencing disruptive change. Foucault understood the need for a place in society where people could safely experience crisis without penalty. He also expressed the concern that the heterotopias of crisis—places of sanctuary and escape—were actually changing in contemporary times to "heterotopias of deviance," social and physical configurations of permanent crisis and liminality.[21] He argues that this gradual change to classifying crisis liminality as deviance presents serious problems, because it is within the space of liminality that individuals are eventually able to effect change.

When societies categorize liminality as pathological, people have little, if any, space to be vulnerable or *in-between*. As my participants indicate, this has severe consequences for them. Because they are socially, psychologically, and physically debilitated from their hardened social and political landscape, it reduces them to conditions that begin to resemble *bare life*. Lacking places of social or political refuge, some drop out of activism and discontinue any further political engagement.

In addition, the attempt to decrease places of refuge by eradicating liminality is physically emphasized by the walling off of communities, homes, nation-states, and identities. However, the effects of walling are deleterious: families are fractured, people unnecessarily die, indigenous populations are divided, and risk factors for violence increase. Although walling may be psychologically comforting, walls allow individuals to contract their awareness and block out the suffering of others. This contraction of awareness is a spell that citizens and political institutions cast upon themselves and each other. It allows individuals to blind themselves to the dangers that these methods of social exclusion pose. Several participants acknowledge this risk when they express that "no one is safe." They recognize that their predicament hinders positive change and transformation. This is why, at the end of his essay, Foucault poetically states that, in societies that lack the necessary places of refuge for individuals experiencing crisis or change, "dreams dry up, espionage takes the place of adventure, and police take the place of pirates."[22] With this quote in mind, the topic of dreams and the act of dreaming will be the focus of my conclusion. Immediately following the next chapter, I will examine dreaming as a conscious act of agency—a space of possibility, transformation, and change.

CHAPTER 6
HARSH REALMS

This chapter is a photographic essay, consisting of twenty images. I consider these images to be social artifacts that illustrate the interaction of ideas, people, material objects, and especially built environments. Because much of what is circulated in the media about Arizona, the borderlands, and its residents is often decontextualized, I have provided a short description for each photograph. With these images I map the physical, social, and political landscapes that border crossers encounter. Each of these landscapes is a harsh realm; they are environments that debilitate, disorient, and expose migrants to the continuing intolerance found within local communities.

Figure 25　Border fortification between El Paso and Ciudad Juarez.

Figure 26   Painting of the Virgen de Guadalupe near the migrant trail in the Sonoran region of Mexico. La Virgen is traditionally known as the protectress of the lowly and disenfranchised.

Figure 27   Roadside shrines.

Figure 28   Roadside shrine with prayer candles.

Figure 29   Used prayer candles next to a roadside shrine.

Figure 30   "Coyotes of Altar." Altar is a town in Sonora, Mexico, that serves as a central station for border crossers.

Figure 31   Border wall (Mexico side) in Nogales.

Figure 32   "Desconocido," the "Unknown" or "Stranger."

**Figure 33   "Boycott U.S.A." written on
border wall (Mexico side) in Nogales.**

**Figure 34 US-Mexico border, the demilitarized
zone on the Tohono O'odham reservation.**

Figure 35 Water placed on known migrant trails on the Tohono O'odham reservation.

Figure 36 Discarded clothing, water, and electrolyte beverage containers on a known lay-up site.

Figure 37   Protesters, May 2009.

Figure 38   Protesters.

Figure 39   Graffiti: "Destroy Everything."

Figure 40   Graffiti: "Resist."

Figure 41   Arrests in a Tucson neighborhood.

Figure 42 "We have a dream … united families, decent wages, documents, education, medical care, peace and justice, decent living, social security, civic participation, community rights and duties."

Figure 43   Graffiti: Virgen de Gualalupe with skeletal face.

Figure 44   Graffiti: Sheriff Joe Arpaio and Governor Jan Brewer. Written on Arpaio's chest pocket is "No Mo Joe."

Conclusion
Envisioning Alternatives

Without boats, dreams dry up.

—*Michel Foucault*

The struggle is inner ... our psyches resemble
the border towns and are populated by the same
people. . . . Rigidity is death.

—*Gloria Anzaldúa*

Throughout this book I have explored how processes of militarization emerge. As Renee described in Chapter 4, it emerges as a social and material "rupture" in the environment. In the conversation between Renee and Piper, they both agree that a "shift" in consciousness needs to happen. This shift requires, my participants observed, "holistic thinking." Such a shift must radically change the social, mental, linguistic, and material landscapes that inform the lives of residents who live in these areas. Yet institutionalized practices of war, and other forms of violence, are extremely difficult to disrupt, and they operate as a powerful psychological enchantment. Participants did, however, hint at one way that individuals attempt to shift their consciousness and break the spell—through dreaming. My conversations with Dean, an activist with Good Neighbors, illustrate this point.

Tucson, Summer 2010

Early one Saturday morning, Dean and I went into the Sonoran Desert. This would be one of my last field trips with the Good Neighbors; we would survey the desert and search for border crossers. While driving through the desert, I mentioned to Dean that some friends of mine had talked about the social and political climate in Arizona as being in need of a "shift in consciousness." Dean furrowed his brow, nodded, and began to offer his perspective on the idea of *consciousness*:

> *Dean:* Consciousness. I think that idea has some validity, because the state of mind that is dictating policy is not working. There has to be a shift in consciousness. The fact that people are dying and starving in the desert here—and it is rarely addressed—is a problem.
>
> *Nicole:* So what does this term *consciousness* actually mean to you?
>
> *Dean:* Total awareness. Being conscious means to really be aware. If not, then the viewpoint focus is really narrow. It's important to understand where other people are coming from, too. I mean, I shouldn't condemn someone for not listening to me if I am not listening to them—where they are coming from, what they are saying. People like to look at this as more of a legal issue—more of an invasion—but they don't really realize how complicated this is. If they sat down at their table and understood where their food came from, where their clothes came from ... [*Dean trailed off.*]
>
> *Nicole:* Is that total awareness?
>
> *Dean:* Yes, that is part of it. I may not make the best decisions, because I don't know all the facts. But I try. But I think that actually going through that thought process is a very good thing. You know, it's like, five years ago I was really in the dark. I didn't know anything that happened about what was going on in the desert here. I never condemn or judge, because I was very ignorant not so long ago. But once I did understand, I couldn't turn my back.
>
> But you know, the funny thing about consciousness ... people like to be part of a group. Groupthink is really powerful. I think people make a conscious effort not to deviate from groupthink. Whether you are part of Good Neighbors, Ya Basta, or part of the Minutemen, there is a conscious effort not to deviate from the group's way of thinking. It's really easy to lose yourself in the groupthink. I don't know if it's a conscious decision

not to be conscious. . . . I just don't know. But it's like that saying, "Be the change you want to see in the world." How can I expect anyone to act a certain way if I don't? That means being civil to the Border Patrol [officers], kind to the migrants. It's like when Martin Luther King talked about the "violence of the spirit." That can really do you in. You don't want to go out with a certain frame of mind that expects conflict. We have to be careful of physical violence, but the violence of the spirit is more dangerous, I think. Because if you have preconceived notions of some thing or someone, it can come to the surface. It doesn't benefit me, it doesn't benefit them, it doesn't benefit Good Neighbors. It doesn't benefit anyone. You've got to be able to dream. Be able to see things differently, you know? People need dreams.

Dean's statement "People need dreams" intrigued me. I began to think about the use of dreams in my own life to solve problems, the narrative of the DREAM Act, and how indigenous scholars approach dreaming. In these final pages, I argue that dreaming—that is, the practice of deliberate envisioning—is a radical act through which individuals re-imagine themselves in an inimical social realm. I contend that dreaming is rarely ever metaphorical; instead, it is a process by which individuals deliberately shift awareness and envision new identities and alternative strategies of survival. I start this chapter with a brief exploration of the basic ideas underlying the DREAM Act. Through the work of Chicana activist Gloria Anzaldúa I then explore what Linda Tuhiwai Smith describes as *envisioning*, a decolonizing strategy among indigenous populations who have experienced the deleterious effects of imperialism on both outer and inner terrains. Finally, I close with an assessment of the consequences of militarization.

The Relief of DREAMing: The Message of the Development, Relief, and Education for Alien Minors Act

In 2001 during the 107th Congress, senators Orrin Hatch and Dick Durbin introduced Senate Bill 1291, the Development, Relief, and Education for Alien Minors (DREAM) Act. This bill was introduced as a bipartisan solution that would "provide undocumented youths who came to the United States before the age of sixteen a path towards legalization on the condition that they attend college or serve in the U.S. military for a minimum of two years while maintaining good moral character."[1] As of February 2013, more than a decade later, the DREAM Act has not been passed into legislation. This bill, stymied by bureaucratic misgivings and popular pressure, is labeled an *amnesty* bill among its detractors. They argue that it rewards the actions of those who migrate illegally to the United States. However, the DREAM Act has also garnered a large number of supporters among humanitarian activists in Arizona and elsewhere in the nation. In January 2013, Senator John McCain of Arizona spoke publicly in support of the DREAM Act and in favor of comprehensive immigration reform. Senator McCain commented, "We can't go on forever with 11 million people living in this country in the shadows in an illegal status. . . . We cannot forever have children who were born here—who were brought here by their parents when they were small children—to live in the shadows, as well."[2]

Even though the DREAM Act has not passed into law, the narrative and the ideas behind it have gained momentum. The aspiring undocumented youth has emerged as a central figure in the narrative of the DREAM Act. The "Dreamer"[3] symbolizes an aspiring young person who undergoes nearly insurmountable odds, desires to assimilate, is hardworking, and has skills to offer. This narrative of dreaming and of being a *dreamer* taps into a mythology that draws upon the vision of the American Dream and Dr. Martin Luther King's visionary appeal in his "I Have a Dream" speech, which he delivered during the height of the civil rights movement. This narrative embodies the creative spirit and drive of individuals who face severe obstacles yet choose to envision and aspire.

Dreaming as a Path of Agency

Dreaming is hardly new; as Tuhiwai Smith and others point out, it is a long-standing practice.[4] Indigenous peoples across time have relied on dreams for problem solving and gathering collective wisdom. Tuhiwai Smith explains that dreaming, or creating a new vision, is a political act and a strategy that "effectively binds people together . . . which asks people to imagine a future, that they rise above present day situations which are generally depressing." Dreaming is a form of sacred creation through which individuals "dream new visions and hold onto old ones. It fosters inventions and discoveries, facilitates simple improvements to people's lives and uplifts our spirits."[5] In other words, dreaming is a space where people can be creative, invent new ways of being in the world, and find space in which to enact one's agency. It is a tool for survival.

Michel Foucault alluded to the danger that society may suffer when individuals are restricted from dreaming when he said, "In civilizations without boats, dreams dry up, espionage takes the place of adventure, and police take the place of pirates."[6] In other words, the boat is a place of refuge and sanctuary for those undergoing crisis and transition. Foucault's observation addresses one of the main threads that I highlighted in Chapter 5: what happens when individuals who experience crisis, suffering, and trials are labeled as *deviant*? He states that individuals need places of refuge and sanctuary where they are allowed to be in crisis without penalty or harm. As a persistently stigmatized population, border crossers lack such sanctuary. The realm in which they enter is organized through binaries, inimical to fluidity, and formulated through static constructions of identity. When individuals identify too closely with these binaries, they participate in a process of contracting their own awareness, thereby fixing their own identity. Consequently, the social and environmental atmosphere is ordered through static notions of self, and thus, new ways of being are limited. When the environment is physically altered to reinforce those ideas, its ideological effects are amplified, and people start to aggregate in camps. This is what Dean described as *groupthink,* the collective force that lies behind the camp mentalities of belonging.

The Border Crosser as Visionary and Decolonizer

More than twenty-five years ago, Gloria Anzaldúa recognized the danger of a static identity; it had a harmful and debilitating effect on individuals whose lives were in flux. Anzaldúa struggled with the difficulties of being subject to the social constructs of identity based in dichotomous thinking. She identified this as an intrinsic aspect of living in the contemporary United States. This was especially challenging for a person who was on the borderlands of identity—she identified as tejana and queer. Anzaldúa called for what she termed a *mestiza consciousness,* a hybrid state of mind that tolerates ambiguity:

> La mestiza constantly has to shift out of habitual formations; from convergent thinking, analytical reasoning that tends to use rationality to move toward a single goal (a Western mode) to divergent thinking, characterized by movement away from set patterns and goals and toward a more whole perspective, one that includes rather than excludes.[7]

Later she explains that the objective of the person who inhabits a *mestiza consciousness* is to "break down the subject-object duality that keeps her a prisoner and to show in the flesh and through the images in her work how duality is transcended."[8]

Anzaldúa also observed that a rigid identity is what enables a *militarized zone* of the self to emerge.[9] Like Dean who observed, "people need dreams," she calls for the breaking down of boundaries and declared "rigidity is death." In a later work, she summons the reader to work toward liberating oneself from rigid categories and to conjure a "new vision," a new way of *conocimiento* (knowing), and to risk being a *nepantlera* (boundary crosser). This act of envisioning—of dreaming—requires that individuals be able to consciously move away from an investment in fixed identities that rely on "power relations that crush citizen-subjects into positionalities." The *nepantlera* actively shifts her perception, intentionally crosses realities, and rejects rigid ideological systems and subjectivities. The act of walking between worlds becomes a radical tool of resistance that destabilizes the power of the state. When individuals consciously struggle against static categories and identities, this becomes a sacred act of boundary crossing and a path to liberation. Thus, border crossing is also viewed as a decolonizing act. Just as Anzaldúa recognized many years ago, my participants confirmed this interpretation; they view the actions of border crossers to be revolutionary and heroic. Interviewees perceive migrants as being able to consciously envision a different life in order to free themselves from oppressive institutions that destroy them and their communities.

States of Injury

Although many participants view border crossers as heroic, they also recognize the actions of crossers as a cry for help. When participants like Dan point to the violence that occurs within their communities and observe that

Figure 45   Neighborhood mural, Tucson.

"no one is safe," they hint at the entrenchment of institutionalized violence within their communities. However, institutionalized violence occurs at the level of the self, when we rely upon fixed, unchangeable identities. Although at first glimpse these positionalities appear to be spaces of agency and self-preservation, they are instruments of statecraft. Alliances based in mechanical solidarity that are preserved at all costs amplify what Dean describes as the "violence of the spirit." These are oppressive and rigid boundaries that condition individuals to be indifferent to the social and physical suffering of others, as well as to their eventual death. Such indifference results in the systematic militarization of entire communities and, as participants describe, places all of its residents at risk for further injury.[10] The proliferation of detention centers, punitive methods of incarceration, racial profiling, and polarized rhetoric evidently exacerbate the suffering of already disenfranchised individuals. As participants confirm, their current communities are militarized and are so inimical to living that it has resulted in their social, psychological, and physical devastation, reducing people to conditions that resemble *bare life*. These communities are the nascent formations of *death worlds*—that is, realms of "social existence in which vast populations are subjected to conditions of life conferring upon them the status of the living dead."[11]

Therefore, I conclude that the social suffering that participants articulate are the social and material consequences of statecraft. Both residents and those who travel through the borderlands live along the fault lines that compose statecraft. They are left in an unceasing state of injury, a condition that permeates their habitats and consumes them both physically and psychologically. Their condition is one that is born out of being borderline—socially, politically, and geographically. What participants described in the preceding pages is the spell of statecraft at work—a pervasive and institutionalized violence that alters an individual's state of consciousness. Such an alteration in awareness reconfigures a person's sense of self and conditions him or her to do the necessary labor required for statecraft; they are trained to be indifferent to the multiple levels of human suffering and destruction.

To close, I ask the question that Dr. King posed in 1967: "Where do we go from here?" Residents of Phoenix and Tucson face this question every day. Militarization relies on the physical and psychical restructuring of one's social world to maintain the image of a powerful nation-state. However, the maintenance of this image comes at a high price. The lives of the undocumented and the documented, of citizens and noncitizens alike, are organized in ways that incite division, emphasize difference, and intentionally create warfare. Participants observe that these attributes appear to be indicators of a nation in despair. They worry that Arizona, a state known for its entangled history and legacies of frontier violence, is the proverbial canary in a coal mine that foreshadows an eventual civil war. If this is the case, the advice from scholars such as Anzaldúa, Foucault, and Gilroy is provident: we need to liberate ourselves from the rigid structures of contemporary notions of identity. They are no longer useful. Instead, individuals must learn how to actively envision new ways of being in order to expand their realm of action. For if we allow ourselves to continue on a path of intolerance and ignore the crises of others, we participate in a soul killing "violence of the spirit." In a radical act of envisioning, Anzaldúa invites each of us to learn how to be fluid, cross boundaries, and reclaim our spirit and humanity, for "rigidity is death."

Notes

Introduction

1. As I write this, approximately 24,668 unaccompanied children have crossed the US-Mexico border. As of June 2, 2014, President Obama has declared this event an "urgent humanitarian situation." See Zezima, Katie, and Ed O'Keefe, "Obama Calls Wave of Children across U.S.-Mexican Border 'Urgent Humanitarian Situation,'" *Washington Post,* June 2, 2014.

2. Bach, Robert, "Transforming Border Security: Prevention First," *Homeland Security Affairs* 1(1), Summer 2005.

3. Tucson Samaritans, "Death in the Desert," www.tucsonsamaritans.org /death-in-the-desert.html. Retrieved June 20, 2013.

4. Although I generally use the terms *border* and *boundary* interchangeably, here I use the term *border* to refer to the physical wall that demarcates the two contiguous political entities, the United States and Mexico. Drawing upon Joseph Nevins's definition, I use *boundary* more loosely to refer to a strict line of separation.

5. Lacey, Mark, "Arizona Officials, Fed up with U.S. Efforts, Seek Donations to Build a Border Fence," *New York Times,* July 19, 2011.

6. Andreas, Peter, *Border Games: Policing the U.S.-Mexico Divide,* Ithaca, NY: Cornell University Press, 2000.

7. Ibid., p. 10.

8. Ibid., p. 12.

9. Ibid., p. 82.

10. Ibid., p. 85.

11. Couliano, Ioan, *Eros and Magic in the Renaissance,* Chicago, IL: University of Chicago Press, 1987.

12. Mbembe, Achille, "Necropolitics," *Public Culture* 15(1): 11–40, 2003.

13. Lutz, Catherine, *Homefront: A Military City and the American 20th Century,* Boston, MA: Beacon Press, 2001.

14. Peña, Devon G., *Mexican Americans and the Environment: Tierra y vida,* Tucson, AZ: University of Tucson Press, 2005.

15. Stoler, Ann Laura, "Imperial Debris: Reflections on Ruin and Ruination," *Cultural Anthropology* 23(2): 192–219, 2008.

16. Žižek, Slavoj, *Violence: Six Sideways Reflections,* New York: Picador Press, 2008.

17. Ibid., p. 11.

18. Ibid.

19. Arizona Department of Administration, "Arizona Department of Administration Announces $735 Million Sale-Leaseback Transaction," www.azdoa.gov /news/011410release.pdf.

20. As I completed my dissertation, on June 20, 2013, senators John Hoeven and John Corker introduced a "bipartisan compromise," a border security and fortification amendment that would add 700 miles of border wall and 21,000 Border Patrol Agents.

21. Enloe, Cynthia, *Maneuvers: The International Politics of Militarizing Women's Lives,* Berkeley: University of California Press, 2001.

22. Orr, Jackie, "The Militarization of Inner Space," *Critical Sociology* 30(2): 451–482, 2004.

23. Althusser, Louis, "Ideology and Ideological State Apparatuses: Notes towards an Investigation," *Lenin and Philosophy and Other Essays,* New York: Monthly Review Press, 1971.

24. To ensure their safety, I have not included any interviews with undocumented migrants.

25. All of my procedures were approved by the University of Washington's Human Subjects Division.

26. Trouillot, Michel-Rolph, *Silencing the Past: Power and the Production of History,* New York: Beacon Press, 1995.

27. Martinot, Steve, *The Rule of Racialization: Class, Identity, Governance,* Philadelphia, PA: Temple University Press, 2003.

28. Gilroy, Paul, *Against Race: Imagining Political Culture beyond the Color Line,* Cambridge, MA: Harvard University Press, 2000.

29. I borrow this descriptor from James Ferguson.

Chapter 1

1. Stelzer, Andrew, "State of Fear: Arizona's Immigrant Crackdown," www .radioproject.org/archive/2008/4608.html. Retrieved November 17, 2008.

2. Newman, Nathan, "A War on Immigrants to Fight the War on Terrorism?" www.commondreams.org/cgi-bin/print.cgi?file=/views0110.html.

3. Lynch, Mona, *Sunbelt Justice: Arizona and the American Transformation of Punishment,* Stanford, CA: Stanford University Press, 2010, p. 4.

4. Schlosser, Eric, "The Prison-Industrial-Complex," *The Atlantic Monthly,* December 1998, p. 54.

5. Eisenhower, Dwight D., "The Military-Industrial Complex" speech, http:// coursesa.matrix.msu.edu/~hst306/documents/indust.html. Retrieved February 7, 2013.

6. Ibid.

7. Ibid., p. 8.

8. Ibid.

9. Ibid.

10. Ibid.

11. Ibid., p. 23.

12. Benton-Cohen, Katherine, *Borderline Americans: Racial Division and Labor War in the Arizona Borderlands,* Cambridge, MA: Harvard University Press, 2009, p. 49.

13. Ibid., p. 52.

14. Ibid.

15. Ibid., p. 54.

16. Ibid., p. 55.

17. Biggers, Jeff, *State out of the Union: Arizona and the Final Showdown over the American Dream,* New York: Nation Books, 2012.

18. Arpaio, Joseph, *America's Toughest Sheriff: How We Can Win the War against Crime,* Arlington, TX: Summit Publishing, 1996, p. 97.

19. Arpaio, Joseph, *Joe's Law: America's Toughest Sheriff Takes on Illegal Immigration, Drugs, and Everything Else That Threatens America,* New York: AMACOM Books, 2008.

20. Stern, Alexandra Minna, *Eugenic Nation: Faults and Frontiers of Better Breeding in Modern America,* Berkeley: University of California Press, 2005.

21. National Archives and Records Administration, "Transcript of Treaty at Guadalupe Hidalgo," www.ourdocuments.gov/doc.php?flash=true&doc=26 &page=transcript. Retrieved February 12, 2013.

22. Benton-Cohen, p. 17.

23. Ibid., p. 77.

24. An extended history of the process of racialization in Arizona is beyond the scope of this book. However, I draw on Benton-Cohen's analysis in order to highlight the social and historical patterns that allow for current events in Arizona to emerge. In addition to the scholars that I draw upon here and in Chapter 2, my discussions of historical processes of racialization and immigration have been influenced by Leo R. Chavez, *The Latino Threat: Constructing Immigrants, Citizens, and the Nation* (Stanford, CA: Stanford University Press, 2008) and José David Saldívar, *Border Matters: Remapping American Cultural Studies* (Berkeley: University of California Press, 1997).

25. Byrkit, James W., "The I.W.W. in Wartime Arizona," www.library.arizona.edu/exhibits/bisbee/docs/jahbyrk.html. Retrieved February 12, 2013.

26. Benton-Cohen, p. 217.

27. Ibid., p. 83.

28. Byrkit.

29. University of Arizona, "The Bisbee Deportation of 1917," www.library.arizona.edu/exhibits/bisbee/docs/jahbyrk.html. Retrieved February 12, 2013.

30. Ibid.

31. Benton-Cohen, *Borderline Americans*, p. 2.

32. Ibid.

33. Biggers, p. 138.

34. Ibid., p. 139.

35. United Farm Workers, "The Story of Cesar Chavez," www.ufw.org/_page.php?menu=research&inc=history/07.html. Retrieved January 12, 2013.

36. Pawel, Miriam, *The Union of Their Dreams: Power, Hope, and Struggle in Cesar Chavez's Farm Worker Movement*, New York: Bloomsbury Press, 2009, p. x.

37. For an extensive history of Cesar Chavez's and the history of the United Farm Workers of America, see ibid. and Pawel's *The Crusades of Cesar Chavez: A Biography* (New York: Bloomsbury Press, 2014).

38. Hacking, Ian, "Making up People," in *Reconstructing Individualism*, ed. Heller, Sosna, and Wellbery, Stanford, CA: Stanford University Press, 1986.

39. Ibid., p. 229.

Chapter 2

1. Tilly, Charles, "War-Making and State-Making as Organized Crime," in *Bringing the State Back In,* ed. Evans, Rueschmeyer, and Skocpol, Cambridge, MA: Cambridge University Press, 1985.

2. Bowman, Glenn, "The Violence in Identity," *Anthropology of Violence and Conflict,* London: Routledge, 2001.

3. Scarry, Elaine, *The Body in Pain: The Making and Unmaking of the World,* Oxford: Oxford University Press, 1985.

4. Brass, Paul, "Elite Competition and Nation-Formation," in *Nationalism,* ed. Hutchinson and Smith, Oxford: Oxford University Press, 1994.

5. I focus more closely on the work of Lipsitz because he is one of the few authors I have found to directly connect the construct of whiteness to the use of war as an extended metaphor in the United States.

6. Lipsitz, George, *The Possessive Investment in Whiteness: How White People Profit from Identity Politics,* Philadelphia, PA: Temple University Press, 1998.

7. Ibid., p. 3.

8. Ibid., p. 24.

9. Ibid., p. 47.

10. Ibid., p. 49.

11. Ibid.

12. Maricopa County Recorder Election Results, http://recorder.maricopa .gov/electionresults/screen5Static.aspx. Retrieved January 19, 2013.

13. Lipsitz, p. 56.

14. When I returned to Phoenix in January 2011 Eric (an activist I introduced earlier in the chapter) informed me that underground networks were beginning to be developed by community members to help migrants with errands and other daily activities in order to reduce their exposure to police scrutiny.

15. Appadurai, Arjun, *Fear of Small Numbers: An Essay on the Geography of Anger,* Durham, NC: Duke University Press, 2006.

16. Ibid., p. 8.

17. Ibid., p. 9.

18. Eagleton, Terry, *Ideology: An Introduction,* London: Verso Press, 1991.

19. See Chapter 1, Arizona and Its "Conditions of Possibility."

20. Brown, Wendy, *Walled States, Waning Sovereignty,* Brooklyn, NY: Zone Books, 2010.

21. Lynch, Mona, *Sunbelt Justice: Arizona and the Transformation of American Punishment,* Stanford, CA: Stanford University Press, 2010.

22. Harvey, David, *The Condition of Postmodernity,* Oxford: Blackwell Publishing, 1990.

23. Ibid., p. 21.

24. Ibid., p. 217.

25. Most recently a discussion of the 99 percent has arisen in response to the banking crisis and the response of the government to subsidize the crisis. This

has been the closest semblance to a public discussion of social stratification by class.

26. Roediger, David, *The Wages of Whiteness: Race and the Making of the American Working Class,* New York: Verso Press, 1991, p. 13.

27. Wray, Matt, *Not Quite White: White Trash and the Boundaries of Whiteness,* Durham, NC: Duke University Press, 2006.

28. Lipsitz, p. 91.

29. Foucault, Michel, *The History of Sexuality, Volume 1: An Introduction,* New York: Vintage Books, 1978.

Chapter 3

1. Simon, Jonathan, *Governing through Crime: How the War on Crime Transformed American Democracy and Created a Culture of Fear,* Oxford: Oxford University Press, 2007.

2. Rose, Nikolas, *Powers of Freedom: Reframing Political Thought,* Cambridge: Cambridge University Press, 1999.

3. For an extended discussion of the political rationalities that are essential to immigration policy and practice, see Jonathan Xavier Inda's *Targeting Immigrants: Government, Technology, and Ethics* (Malden, MA: Blackwell, 2006).

4. Rose, p. 259.

5. Garland, David, *The Culture of Control: Crime and Social Order in a Contemporary Society,* Chicago, IL: University of Chicago Press, 2001.

6. Rose, p. 88.

7. Gilmore, Ruth Wilson, *Golden Gulag: Prisons, Surplus, Crisis, and Opposition in Globalizing California,* Berkeley: University of California Press, 2007.

8. Ferguson, James, *The Anti-Politics Machine: "Development," Depoliticization, and Bureaucratic Power in Lesotho,* Minneapolis: University of Minnesota Press, 1994.

9. Hacking, Ian, *Historical Ontology,* Cambridge, MA: Harvard University Press, 2004.

10. Ferguson, p. 267.

11. Gilmore, p. 27.

12. Ibid., p. 179.

13. Ferguson, p. 88.

Chapter 4

1. Oxford Online English Dictionary. Retrieved December 2012.

2. Cauwels, Janet, *Imbroglio: Rising to the Challenges of Borderline Personality Disorder*, New York: W. W. Norton and Company, 1992, p. 26.

3. In the days after the shooting in Tucson, another branch of discussion (originating especially from media pundits) revolved around individuals suffering from a mental illness and their easy access to guns. Although mental illness and access to guns do partially contribute, the incidents in Arizona acquire a specific, local shape that sets the conditions of possibility for acts of violence like these to occur.

4. I did not have the opportunity to interview Shawna Forde or Jared Loughner. This is clearly a limitation of this chapter.

5. Andreas, Peter, *Border Games: Policing the U.S.-Mexico Divide*, Ithaca, NY: Cornell University Press, 2000.

6. Nevins, Joseph, *Operation Gatekeeper: The Rise of the "Illegal Alien" and the Making of the U.S.-Mexico Boundary*, New York: Routledge Press, 2002.

7. Linehan, Marsha M., *Cognitive Behavioral Treatment of Borderline Personality Disorder*, New York: The Guilford Press, 1993, p. 18.

8. Oxford English Dictionary, www.oed.com/view/Entry/51885?redirected From=dialectical#eid. Retrieved January 12, 2013.

9. Cauwels.

10. Bateson, Gregory, *Steps to an Ecology of Mind*, New York: Ballantine Books, 1972.

11. Cauwels, p. 345.

12. Linehan, p. 31.

13. Ibid., p. 32.

14. Ibid., p. 36.

15. Ibid.

16. Low, Setha, *Behind the Gates: Life, Security, and the Pursuit of Happiness in Fortress America*, New York: Routledge Press, 2004.

17. McKinley, Jesse, "New Border Fear: Violence by a Rogue Militia," *New York Times*, June 26, 2009.

18. Retrieved from Justice for Shawna Forde website, www.justiceforshawn aforde.com/write-shawna. Retrieved January 13, 2013.

19. Anderson, Rick, "Lethally Blonde," *Seattle Weekly*, July 15, 2009.

20. Ibid.

21. Lonnie Athens quoted in Rhodes, Richard, *Why They Kill: The Discoveries of a Maverick Criminologist*, New York: Vintage Books, 1999. p. 136.

22. Athens in ibid., p. 112.

23. Athens in ibid.

24. A narrative of Shawna Forde's formative years and the events that took place

in Arivaca are chronicled by David Neiwert in *And Hell Followed with Her: Crossing the Dark Side of the American Border* (New York: Nation Books, 2013).

25. Turner, Victor, *Dramas, Fields, and Metaphors: Symbolic Action in Human Society,* Ithaca, NY: Cornell University Press, 1974.

26. Paradis, Cheryl, "The Measure of Madness," *Psychology Today* blog, www.psychologytoday.com/blog/the-measure-madness/201102/shawna-forde-sentenced-death.

27. Anderson.

28. Wielemans, Sebastien, "A Cycle of Fences," http://vimeo.com/20137911. Retrieved January 13, 2013.

29. Woodward, Ian, *Understanding Material Culture,* London: Sage Publications, 2007, p. 3.

30. Ibid., p. 6.

31. Wray, p. 3.

32. Scarry, Elaine, *The Body in Pain: The Making and Unmaking of the World,* Oxford: Oxford University Press, 1985.

33. Douglas, Mary, *Purity and Danger: An Analysis on the Concepts of Pollution and Taboo,* London: Routledge Press, 1966.

34. Sundberg, Juanita, "'Trash-Talk' and the Production of Quotidian Geopolitical Boundaries in the USA-Mexico Borderlands," *Social and Cultural Geography* 9(8), December 2008.

35. I further explore Sundberg's discussion of trash in Chapter 5.

36. Herrenkohl, Todd, and Eugene Aisenberg, "The Context of Violence," in *Violence in Context: Current Evidence on Risk, Protection, and Prevention,* ed. Herrenkohl et al., Oxford: Oxford University Press, 2011.

37. Miller, Laura, "The Real Message of Loughner's Book List," www.salon.com/2011/01/10/loughner_book_list/. Retrieved January 13, 2013.

38. Ibid.

39. Ibid.

40. Lipton, Eric, Charlie Savage, and Scott Shane, "Arizona Suspect's Recent Acts Offer Hints of Alienation," *New York Times,* January 8, 2011.

41. Baumann, Nick, "Loughner Friend Explains Alleged Gunman's Grudge against Giffords," *Mother Jones,* January 10, 2011. www.motherjones.com/politics/2011/01/jared-lee-loughner-friend-voicemail-phone-message. Retrieved January 10, 2013.

Chapter 5

1. Agamben, Giorgio, *Homo Sacer: Sovereign Power and Bare Life,* Stanford, CA: Stanford University Press, 1998, pp. 168–169.

2. Gilroy, Paul, *Against Race: Imagining Political Culture beyond the Color Line*, Cambridge, MA: Harvard University Press, 2000, p. 71.

3. Agamben, p. 166.

4. Douglas, Mary, *Purity and Danger: An Analysis on the Concepts of Pollution and Taboo*, London: Routledge and Kegan Paul, 1966.

5. Agamben, p. 166.

6. Gilroy, p. 83.

7. Ibid., p. 87.

8. Ibid., p. 71.

9. Agamben, p. 170.

10. Ibid., p. 1.

11. Tohono O'odham Nation, "We:s T-We:m 'am B O Ju: Together We Will," www.tonation-nsn.gov/history_culture.aspx. Retrieved April 24, 2013.

12. De León, Jason P., "'Better to Be Hot Than Caught': Excavating the Conflicting Roles of Migrant Material Culture," *American Anthropologist* 114(3): 477–495, 2012.

13. Sundberg, Juanita, "'Trash-Talk' and the Production of Quotidian Geopolitical Boundaries in the USA-Mexico Borderlands," *Social and Cultural Geography* 9(8), December 2008.

14. Feeley, Malcolm M., and Jonathan Simon, "The New Penology: Notes on the Emerging Strategy of Corrections and Its Implication," *Criminology* 30(4): 449–474, 1992.

15. Low, Setha, *Behind the Gates: Life, Security, and the Pursuit of Happiness in Fortress America,* New York: Routledge Press, 2004, p. 138.

16. Ibid., p. 139.

17. For example, in January 2009, the National Geographic Channel launched a docuseries entitled *Border Wars*. A commentator for the *Huffington Post* described the series as operating "at the expense of the worst humanitarian crisis occurring on US soil today" and that it "appeals to the lowest common denominator. It blatantly plays stereotypes and stokes fears to push profits." See "National Geographic Channel Profits from Humanitarian Crisis," www.huffingtonpost.com/john-carlos-frey /national-geographic-chann_b_428624.html. Retrieved January 11, 2013.

18. Turner, Victor, *Dramas, Fields, and Metaphors: Symbolic Action in Human Society*, Ithaca, NY: Cornell University Press, 1974.

19. Agamben, Giorgio, *State of Exception,* Chicago, IL: University of Chicago Press, 2007, p. 1.

20. Foucault, Michel, "Of Other Spaces," *Diacritics* 16(1): Spring 1986, p. 27.

21. Ibid., p. 25.

22. Ibid., p. 27.

Conclusion

1. North American Integration and Development Center, "No DREAMers Left Behind: The Economic Potential of DREAM Act Beneficiaries," http://naid .ucla.edu/uploads/4/2/1/9/4219226/no_dreamers_left_behind.pdf. Retrieved March 4, 2013.

2. Wilkie, Christina, "John McCain on Immigration Reform: Path to Citizenship, Dream Act Must Be Included," *Huffington Post,* www .huffingtonpost.com/2013/01/27/john-mccain-immigration-reform_n _2561614.html#slide=more232319. Retrieved March 5, 2013.

3. Lopez, William D., et al., "Boundaries in the Lives of Undocumented Immigrants," *Anthropology News,* January/February 2013.

4. Tuhiwai Smith, Linda, *Decolonizing Methodologies: Research and Indigenous Peoples,* New York: Palgrave/St. Martin's Press, 2008.

5. Ibid., p. 158.

6. Foucault, Michel, "Of Other Spaces," *Diacritics* 16(1): Spring 1986, p. 27.

7. Anzaldúa, Gloria, *Borderlands/La Frontera: The New Mestiza,* San Francisco, CA: Aunt Lute Books, 1987.

8. Ibid., p. 102.

9. Anzaldúa, Gloria, "now let us shift ... the path of conocimiento ... inner work, public acts," *this bridge we call home: radical visions for transformation,* New York: Routledge, 2002.

10. A recent article in the *American Journal of Public Health* highlights war as a public health issue and identifies "the many manifestations of militarism ... illustrate the pervasive and pernicious nature of fundamental causes, and emphasize the need for greater public health efforts to prevent war." See Wiist, William, Kathy Barker, Neil Arya, Jon Rohde, Martin Donohue, Shelley White, Pauline Lubens, Geraldine Gorman, and Amy Hagopian, "The Role of Public Health in the Prevention of War: Rationale and Competencies," *American Journal of Public Health* 104(6): e34–e47, June 2014.

11. Mbembe, Achille, "Necropolitics," *Public Culture* 15(1): 11–40, 2003, p. 40.

BIBLIOGRAPHY

Agamben, Giorgio. *State of Exception*. Chicago, IL: University of Chicago Press, 2007.

———. *Homo Sacer: Sovereign Power and Bare Life*. Stanford, CA: Stanford University Press, 1998.

Althusser, Louis. "Ideology and Ideological State Apparatuses: Notes towards an Investigation." *Lenin and Philosophy and Other Essays*. New York: Monthly Review Press, 1971.

Anderson, Rick. "Lethally Blonde." *Seattle Weekly*, July 15, 2009.

Andreas, Peter. *Border Games: Policing the U.S.-Mexico Divide*. Ithaca, NY: Cornell University Press, 2000.

Anzaldúa, Gloria. "now let us shift … the path of conocimiento … inner work, public acts." *this bridge we call home: radical visions for transformation*. New York: Routledge, 2002.

———. *Borderlands/La Frontera: The New Mestiza*. San Francisco, CA: Aunt Lute Books, 1987.

Appadurai, Arjun. *Fear of Small Numbers: An Essay on the Geography of Anger*. Durham, NC: Duke University Press, 2006.

Arizona Department of Administration. "Arizona Department of Administration Announces $735 Million Sale-Leaseback Transaction." www.azdoa.gov/news/011410release.pdf.

Arpaio, Joseph. *Joe's Law: America's Toughest Sheriff Takes on Illegal Immigration, Drugs, and Everything Else That Threatens America*. New York: AMACOM Books, 2008.

————. *America's Toughest Sheriff: How We Can Win the War against Crime.* Arlington, TX: Summit Publishing, 1996.

Bach, Robert. "Transforming Border Security: Prevention First." *Homeland Security Affairs* 1(1), Summer 2005.

Bateson, Gregory. *Steps to an Ecology of Mind.* New York: Ballantine Books, 1972.

Baumann, Nick. "Loughner Friend Explains Alleged Gunman's Grudge against Giffords." *Mother Jones,* January 10, 2011.

Benton-Cohen, Katherine. *Borderline Americans: Racial Division and Labor War in the Arizona Borderlands.* Cambridge, MA: Harvard University Press, 2009.

Biggers, Jeff. *State out of the Union: Arizona and the Final Showdown over the American Dream.* New York: Nation Books, 2012.

Bowman, Glenn. "The Violence in Identity." In *Anthropology of Violence and Conflict,* pp. 25–46. London: Routledge, 2001.

Brass, Paul. "Elite Competition and Nation-Formation." In *Nationalism,* ed. John. Hutchinson and Anthony D. Smith, pp. 83–89. Oxford: Oxford University Press, 1994.

Brown, Wendy. *Walled States, Waning Sovereignty.* Brooklyn, NY: Zone Books, 2010.

Byrkit, James W. "The I.W.W. in Wartime Arizona." www.library.arizona .edu/exhibits/bisbee/docs/jahbyrk.html. Retrieved February 12, 2013.

Chavez, Leo R. *The Latino Threat: Constructing Immigrants, Citizens, and the Nation.* Stanford, CA: Stanford University Press, 2008.

Cauwels, Janet. *Imbroglio: Rising to the Challenges of Borderline Personality Disorder.* New York: W. W. Norton and Company, 1992.

Couliano, Ioan. *Eros and Magic in the Renaissance.* Chicago, IL: University of Chicago Press, 1987.

De León, Jason P. "'Better to Be Hot Than Caught': Excavating the Conflicting Roles of Migrant Material Culture." *American Anthropologist* 114(3): 477–495, 2012.

Douglas, Mary. *Purity and Danger: An Analysis of the Concepts of Pollution and Taboo.* London: Routledge Press, 1966.

Eagleton, Terry. *Ideology: An Introduction.* London: Verso Press, 1991.

Eisenhower, Dwight D. "The Military-Industrial Complex" speech. http:// coursesa.matrix.msu.edu/~hst306/documents/indust.html. Retrieved February 7, 2013.

Enloe, Cynthia. *Maneuvers: The International Politics of Militarizing Women's Lives.* Berkeley: University of California Press, 2001.

Feeley, Malcolm M., and Jonathan Simon. "The New Penology: Notes on the Emerging Strategy of Corrections and Its Implication." *Criminology* 30, 1992.

Ferguson, James. *The Anti-Politics Machine: "Development," Depoliticization, and Bureaucratic Power in Lesotho.* Minneapolis: University of Minnesota Press, 1994.

Foucault, Michel. "Of Other Spaces." *Diacritics* 16(1): 22–27, 1986.

———. *The History of Sexuality, Volume 1: An Introduction.* New York: Vintage Books, 1978.

Frey, John Carlos. "National Geographic Channel Profits from Humanitarian Crisis." www.huffingtonpost.com/john-carlos-frey/national -geographic-chann_b_428624.html. Retrieved July 10, 2014.

Garland, David. *The Culture of Control: Crime and Social Order in a Contemporary Society.* Chicago, IL: University of Chicago Press, 2001.

Gilmore, Ruth Wilson. *Golden Gulag: Prisons, Surplus, Crisis, and Opposition in Globalizing California.* Berkeley: University of California Press, 2007.

Gilroy, Paul. *Against Race: Imagining Political Culture beyond the Color Line.* Cambridge, MA: Harvard University Press, 2000.

Hacking, Ian. *Historical Ontology.* Cambridge, MA: Harvard University Press, 2004.

———. "Making up People." In *Reconstructing Individualism,* ed. Thomas Heller, Morton Sosna, and David E. Wellbery, pp. 222–236. Stanford, CA: Stanford University Press, 1986.

Harvey, David. *The Condition of Postmodernity.* Oxford: Blackwell Publishing, 1990.

Herrenkohl, Todd, and Eugene Aisenberg. "The Context of Violence." In *Violence in Context: Current Evidence on Risk, Protection, and Prevention,* ed. Todd Herrenkohl, Eugene Aisenburg, James Herbert Williams, and Jeffrey M. Jenson, pp. 5–11. Oxford: Oxford University Press, 2011.

Inda, Jonathan Xavier. *Targeting Immigrants: Government, Technology, and Ethics.* Malden, MA: Blackwell, 2006.

Lacey, Mark. "Arizona Officials, Fed up with U.S. Efforts, Seek Donations to Build a Border Fence." *New York Times,* July 19, 2011.

Linehan, Marsha M. *Cognitive Behavioral Treatment of Borderline Personality Disorder.* New York: The Guilford Press, 1993.

Lipsitz, George. *The Possessive Investment in Whiteness: How White People*

Profit from Identity Politics. Philadelphia, PA: Temple University Press, 1998.

Lipton, Eric, Charlie Savage, and Scott Shane. "Arizona Suspect's Recent Acts Offer Hints of Alienation." *New York Times,* January 8, 2011.

Lopez, William D., et al. "Boundaries in the Lives of Undocumented Immigrants." *Anthropology News,* January/February 2013.

Low, Setha. *Behind the Gates: Life, Security, and the Pursuit of Happiness in Fortress America*. New York: Routledge Press, 2004.

Lutz, Catherine. *Homefront: A Military City and the American 20th Century*. Boston, MA: Beacon Press, 2001.

Lynch, Mona. *Sunbelt Justice: Arizona and the American Transformation of Punishment*. Stanford, CA: Stanford University Press, 2010.

Maricopa County Recorder Election Results. http://recorder.maricopa .gov/electionresults/screen5Static.aspx. Retrieved January 19, 2013.

Martinot, Steve. *The Rule of Racialization: Class, Identity, Governance*. Philadelphia, PA: Temple University Press, 2003.

Mbembe, Achille. "Necropolitics." *Public Culture* 15(1): 11–40, 2003.

McKinley, Jesse. "New Border Fear: Violence by a Rogue Militia." *New York Times,* June 26, 2009.

Miller, Laura. "The Real Message of Loughner's Book List." www.salon .com/2011/01/10/loughner_book_list/. Retrieved January 13, 2013.

National Archives and Records Administration. "Transcript of Treaty at Guadalupe Hidalgo." www.ourdocuments.gov/doc.php?flash=true &doc=26&page=transcript. Retrieved February 12, 2013.

Neiwert, David. *And Hell Followed with Her: Crossing the Dark Side of the American Border*. New York: Nation Books, 2013.

Nevins, Joseph. *Operation Gatekeeper: The Rise of the "Illegal Alien" and the Making of the U.S.-Mexico Boundary*. New York: Routledge Press, 2002.

Newman, Nathan. "A War on Immigrants to Fight the War on Terrorism?" www.commondreams.org/cgi-bin/print.cgi?file=/views0110.html. Retrieved December 22, 2012.

North American Integration and Development Center. "No DREAMers Left Behind: The Economic Potential of DREAM Act Beneficiaries." http://naid.ucla.edu/uploads/4/2/1/9/4219226/no_dreamers _left_behind.pdf. Retrieved March 4, 2013.

Orr, Jackie. "The Militarization of Inner Space." *Critical Sociology* 30(2): 451–482, 2004.

Paradis, Cheryl. "The Measure of Madness." *Psychology Today* blog. www

.psychologytoday.com/blog/the-measure-madness/201102/shawna
-forde-sentenced-death.

Pawel, Miriam. *The Crusades of Cesar Chavez: A Biography.* New York: Bloomsbury Press, 2014.

———. *The Union of Their Dreams: Power, Hope, and Struggle in Cesar Chavez's Farm Worker Movement.* New York: Bloomsbury Press, 2009.

Peña, Devon G. *Mexican Americans and the Environment: Tierra y vida.* Tucson, AZ: University of Tucson Press, 2005.

Rhodes, Richard. *Why They Kill: The Discoveries of a Maverick Criminologist.* New York: Vintage Books, 1999.

Roediger, David. *The Wages of Whiteness: Race and the Making of the American Working Class.* New York: Verso Press, 1991.

Rose, Nikolas. *Powers of Freedom: Reframing Political Thought.* Cambridge, MA: Cambridge University Press, 1999.

Saldívar, José David. *Border Matters: Remapping American Cultural Studies.* Berkeley: University of California Press, 1997.

Scarry, Elaine. *The Body in Pain: The Making and Unmaking of the World.* Oxford: Oxford University Press, 1985.

Schlosser, Eric. "The Prison-Industrial-Complex." *The Atlantic Monthly,* December 1998.

Simon, Jonathan. *Governing through Crime: How the War on Crime Transformed American Democracy and Created a Culture of Fear.* Oxford: Oxford University Press, 2007.

Stelzer, Andrew. "State of Fear: Arizona's Immigrant Crackdown." National Radio Project. www.radioproject.org/archive/2008/4608.html. Retrieved November 17, 2008.

Stern, Alexandra Minna. *Eugenic Nation: Faults and Frontiers of Better Breeding in Modern America.* Berkeley: University of California Press, 2005.

Stoler, Ann Laura. "Imperial Debris: Reflections on Ruin and Ruination." *Cultural Anthropology* 23(2): 192–219, 2008.

Sundberg, Juanita. "'Trash-Talk' and the Production of Quotidian Geopolitical Boundaries in the USA-Mexico Borderlands." *Social and Cultural Geography* 9(8): 871–890, December 2008.

Tilly, Charles. "War-Making and State-Making as Organized Crime." In *Bringing the State Back In,* ed. Peter B. Evans, Dietrich Rueschmeyer, and Theda Skocpol, pp. 169–190. Cambridge: Cambridge University Press, 1985.

Tohono O'odham Nation. "We:s T-We:m 'am B O Ju: Together We Will." www.tonation-nsn.gov/history_culture.aspx. Retrieved April 24, 2013.

Trouillot, Michel-Rolph. *Silencing the Past: Power and the Production of History.* New York: Beacon Press, 1995.

Tucson Samaritans. "Death in the Desert." www.tucsonsamaritans.org /death-in-the-desert.html. Retrieved June 20, 2013.

Tuhiwai Smith, Linda. *Decolonizing Methodologies: Research and Indigenous Peoples.* New York: Palgrave/St. Martin's Press, 2008.

Turner, Victor. *Dramas, Fields, and Metaphors: Symbolic Action in Human Society.* Ithaca, NY: Cornell University Press, 1974.

United Farm Workers. "The Story of Cesar Chavez." www.ufw.org/_page .php?menu=research&inc=history/07.html. Retrieved January 12, 2013.

University of Arizona. "The Bisbee Deportation of 1917." www.library.arizona .edu/exhibits/bisbee/docs/jahbyrk.html. Retrieved February 12, 2013.

Wielemans, Sebastien. "A Cycle of Fences." http://vimeo.com/20137911. Retrieved January 13, 2013.

Wiist, William, Kathy Barker, Neil Arya, Jon Rohde, Martin Donohue, Shelley White, Pauline Lubens, Geraldine Gorman, and Amy Hagopian. "The Role of Public Health in the Prevention of War: Rationale and Competencies." *American Journal of Public Health* 104(6): e34–e47, June 2014.

Wilkie, Christina. "John McCain on Immigration Reform: Path to Citizenship, Dream Act Must Be Included." *Huffington Post.* www .huffingtonpost.com/2013/01/27/john-mccain-immigration -reform_n_2561614.html#slide=more232319. Retrieved March 5, 2013.

Woodward, Ian. *Understanding Material Culture.* London: Sage Publications, 2007.

Wray, Matt. *Not Quite White: White Trash and the Boundaries of Whiteness.* Durham, NC: Duke University Press, 2006.

Zezima, Katie, and Ed O'Keefe. "Obama Calls Wave of Children across U.S.-Mexican Border 'Urgent Humanitarian Situation.'" *Washington Post,* June 2, 2014.

Žižek, Slavoj. *Violence: Six Sideways Reflections.* New York: Picador Press, 2008.

INDEX